AF767870

RETIREMENT ISSUES, PLANS AND LIFESTYLES

MARRIAGE AND RETIREMENT SECURITY

TRENDS AND IMPLICATIONS

RETIREMENT ISSUES, PLANS AND LIFESTYLES

Additional books in this series can be found on Nova's website under the Series tab.

Additional e-books in this series can be found on Nova's website under the e-book tab.

RETIREMENT ISSUES, PLANS AND LIFESTYLES

MARRIAGE AND RETIREMENT SECURITY

TRENDS AND IMPLICATIONS

IAN M. STYLES
EDITOR

nova publishers
New York

Copyright © 2014 by Nova Science Publishers, Inc.

All rights reserved. No part of this book may be reproduced, stored in a retrieval system or transmitted in any form or by any means: electronic, electrostatic, magnetic, tape, mechanical photocopying, recording or otherwise without the written permission of the Publisher.

For permission to use material from this book please contact us:
Telephone 631-231-7269; Fax 631-231-8175
Web Site: http://www.novapublishers.com

NOTICE TO THE READER

The Publisher has taken reasonable care in the preparation of this book, but makes no expressed or implied warranty of any kind and assumes no responsibility for any errors or omissions. No liability is assumed for incidental or consequential damages in connection with or arising out of information contained in this book. The Publisher shall not be liable for any special, consequential, or exemplary damages resulting, in whole or in part, from the readers' use of, or reliance upon, this material. Any parts of this book based on government reports are so indicated and copyright is claimed for those parts to the extent applicable to compilations of such works.

Independent verification should be sought for any data, advice or recommendations contained in this book. In addition, no responsibility is assumed by the publisher for any injury and/or damage to persons or property arising from any methods, products, instructions, ideas or otherwise contained in this publication.

This publication is designed to provide accurate and authoritative information with regard to the subject matter covered herein. It is sold with the clear understanding that the Publisher is not engaged in rendering legal or any other professional services. If legal or any other expert assistance is required, the services of a competent person should be sought. FROM A DECLARATION OF PARTICIPANTS JOINTLY ADOPTED BY A COMMITTEE OF THE AMERICAN BAR ASSOCIATION AND A COMMITTEE OF PUBLISHERS.

Additional color graphics may be available in the e-book version of this book.

Library of Congress Cataloging-in-Publication Data

ISBN: 978-1-63321-120-9

Published by Nova Science Publishers, Inc. † New York

CONTENTS

PREFACE

Marriage has historically helped protect the financial health of couples and surviving spouses in old age. Based on their marriage, and independent of their own work history, spouses may receive retirement and survivor income through Social Security and some employer-sponsored pension plans. Many of the federal requirements governing these benefits were developed at a time when family structures, work patterns, and pensions were very different from what they are today. In recent decades, marriage has become less common, more households have two earners rather than one, and many employers have shifted from DB plans to DC plans. This book examines the trends in and status of marriage and labor force participation in American households; how those trends have affected spousal benefits and retirement savings behavior within households today; and the implications of these trends for future retirement security.

Chapter 1 - Marriage has historically helped protect the financial health of couples and surviving spouses in old age. Based on their marriage, and independent of their own work history, spouses may receive retirement and survivor income through Social Security and some employer-sponsored pension plans. Many of the federal requirements governing these benefits were developed at a time when family structures, work patterns, and pensions were very different from what they are today. In recent decades, marriage has become less common, more households have two earners rather than one, and many employers have shifted from DB plans to DC plans. In light of these trends, GAO was asked to examine the issue of marriage and retirement security. Specifically, GAO examined: (1) the trends in and status of marriage and labor force participation in American households, (2) how those trends have affected spousal benefits and retirement savings behavior within households today, and (3) the implications of these trends for future retirement security. GAO analyzed nationally representative survey data including the Survey of Consumer Finances, the Survey of Income and Program Participation, and the Current Population Survey (CPS); conducted a broad literature review; and interviewed agency officials and a range of experts in the area of retirement security.

GAO is making no recommendations. GAO received technical comments on a draft of this report from the Department of Labor and the Department of the Treasury, and incorporated them, as appropriate.

Chapter 2 - The Social Security program began in the 1930s and has been modified by Congress many times over the past seven decades. Today, Social Security provides monthly cash benefits to retired or disabled workers and their family members, and to the family members of deceased workers. Among the beneficiary population, approximately 81% are retired or disabled workers, and 19% are the family members of retired, disabled, or deceased workers. In November 2013, 57.9 million beneficiaries received a total of $67 billion in benefit payments for the month. The average benefit payment was $1,164.

Workers become eligible for Social Security benefits for themselves and their family members by working in Social Security-covered employment. An estimated 93% of workers in paid employment or self-employment are covered, and their earnings are subject to the Social Security payroll tax. In 2014, employers and employees each pay 6.2% of covered earnings, up to the annual limit on taxable earnings ($117,000 in 2014).

To be eligible for a Social Security retired-worker benefit, a person generally needs at least 40 earnings credits, or 10 years of Social Security-covered employment (among other requirements). Fewer earnings credits are needed for a disabled-worker benefit, depending on the worker's age. A worker's initial monthly benefit is based on his or her career-average earnings in covered employment. Social Security retired-worker benefits are first payable at the age of 62, subject to a permanent reduction for early retirement. Full (or unreduced) retirement benefits are first payable at the full retirement age (FRA), which is increasing gradually from 65 to 67 under a law enacted by Congress in 1983. The FRA will reach 67 for persons born in 1960 or later (i.e., persons who become eligible for retirement benefits at the age of 62 in 2022 or later).

In addition to payroll taxes, Social Security is financed by federal income taxes that some beneficiaries pay on a portion of their benefits and by interest income that is earned on the Treasury securities held by the Social Security trust funds. In 2012, the Social Security trust funds had receipts totaling $840 billion, expenditures totaling $786 billion, and accumulated assets (in the form of Treasury securities) totaling $2.7 trillion. Projections by the Social Security Board of Trustees show that, based on the program's current financing and benefit structure, benefits scheduled under current law can be paid in full and on time until 2033. The projections also show that Social Security expenditures will exceed income by about 20% *on average* over the next 75 years. Restoring long-range trust fund solvency and other policy objectives have made Social Security reform an issue of ongoing congressional interest and debate.

This report provides an overview of Social Security financing and benefits under current law. Specifically, the report covers the origins and a brief history of the program; Social Security financing and the status of the trust funds; how Social Security benefits are computed; the types of Social Security benefits available to workers and their family members; the basic eligibility requirements for each type of benefit; the scheduled increase in the Social Security retirement age enacted in 1983; and the federal income taxation of Social Security benefits.

In: Marriage and Retirement Security
Editor: Ian M. Styles
ISBN: 978-1-63321-120-9
© 2014 Nova Science Publishers, Inc.

Chapter 1

RETIREMENT SECURITY: TRENDS IN MARRIAGE AND WORK PATTERNS MAY INCREASE ECONOMIC VULNERABILITY FOR SOME RETIREES*

United States Government Accountability Office

WHY GAO DID THIS STUDY

Marriage has historically helped protect the financial health of couples and surviving spouses in old age. Based on their marriage, and independent of their own work history, spouses may receive retirement and survivor income through Social Security and some employer-sponsored pension plans. Many of the federal requirements governing these benefits were developed at a time when family structures, work patterns, and pensions were very different from what they are today. In recent decades, marriage has become less common, more households have two earners rather than one, and many employers have shifted from DB plans to DC plans. In light of these trends, GAO was asked to examine the issue of marriage and retirement security. Specifically, GAO examined: (1) the trends in and status of marriage and labor force participation in American households, (2) how those trends have affected spousal benefits

* This is an edited, reformatted and augmented version of United States Government Accountability Office Publication, No. GAO-14-33, dated January 2014.

and retirement savings behavior within households today, and (3) the implications of these trends for future retirement security. GAO analyzed nationally representative survey data including the Survey of Consumer Finances, the Survey of Income and Program Participation, and the Current Population Survey (CPS); conducted a broad literature review; and interviewed agency officials and a range of experts in the area of retirement security.

GAO is making no recommendations. GAO received technical comments on a draft of this report from the Department of Labor and the Department of the Treasury, and incorporated them, as appropriate.

WHAT GAO FOUND

Over the last 50 years, the composition and work patterns of the American household have changed dramatically. During this period, the proportion of unmarried and never-married individuals in the population increased steadily as couples chose to marry at later ages and live together prior to marriage. At the same time, the proportion of single-parent households more than doubled. These trends were more pronounced for individuals with lower levels of income and education and for certain racial and ethnic groups. Over the same period, labor force participation among married women nearly doubled.

Taken together, these trends have resulted in a decline in the receipt of spousal and survivor benefits and married women contributing more to household retirement savings. From 1960 through 2011, the percentage of women aged 62 and older receiving Social Security benefits based purely on their spouse's (or deceased spouse's) work record declined from 56 to 25. At the same time, the percentage of women receiving benefits based purely on their own work records rose from 39 to 48.

Further, as of 2010, among married households receiving pensions, 40 percent had elected not to receive a survivor benefit. Rising labor force participation among married women enabled them to contribute more to household retirement savings. From 1992 to 2010, married women's average contributions to household retirement savings increased from 20 to 38 percent.

In the future, fewer retirees will receive spousal or survivor benefits from Social Security and private employer-sponsored pension plans, increasing vulnerabilities for some.

Eligibility for Social Security spousal benefits among women is projected to decline, in part, because fewer women are expected to qualify based on marital history and more are expected to qualify for their own benefit based on their own work record. For many women, this shift will be positive, reflecting their greater earnings and capacity to save for retirement. However, women with low levels of lifetime earnings and no spouse or spousal benefit may face greater risk of poverty in old age. For private plans, the shift from defined benefit (DB) to defined contribution (DC) plans increases the vulnerability of spouses because of different federal protections for spouses under these plans.

DB plans are required to offer survivor benefits, which can only be waived with spousal consent. In contrast, DC plan participants generally do not need spousal consent to withdraw funds from the account.

ABBREVIATIONS

BLS	Bureau of Labor Statistics
Census	U.S. Census Bureau
CPS	Current Population Survey
DB	defined benefit
DC	defined contribution
DOMA	Defense of Marriage Act
ERISA	Employee Retirement Income Security Act of 1974
Federal Reserve	Board of Governors of the Federal Reserve System
IPUMS	Integrated Public Use Microdata Series
IRA	individual retirement account
IRC	Internal Revenue Code
QDRO	qualified domestic relations order
QJSA	qualified joint and survivor annuity
QPSA	qualified preretirement survivor annuity
MINT6	Modeling Income in the Near Term model, Version 6
SCF	Survey of Consumer Finances
SIPP	Survey of Income and Program Participation
SSA	Social Security Administration

January 15, 2014

The Honorable Bill Nelson
Chairman
Special Committee on Aging
United States Senate

Dear Chairman Nelson:

Historically, the institution of marriage has served to help protect the financial health of couples, especially couples and surviving spouses in old age. Indeed, based on their marriage, spouses may receive retirement and survivor income from Social Security and some employer-sponsored pension plans.[1] More specifically, Social Security retirement benefits—the most common type of retirement income—are available to individuals who are spouses, widows/widowers, and in some cases former spouses, of workers who qualify for Social Security retirement benefits based on their work history. In addition, private sector defined benefit (DB) plans are required by federal law to include a survivor's benefit for spouses.[2]

However, many of the policies governing spousal retirement benefits were developed at a time when family structures, labor force participation patterns, and retirement plans were very different than they are today. In recent decades, marriage has become less common, and for those who do marry, it is common for both spouses to work. Further, private sector employers have shifted away from DB plans to defined contribution (DC) plans, which generally confer fewer benefits for spouses.[3]

Given these trends, the Senate Special Committee on Aging requested that GAO examine the issue of marriage and retirement security. Specifically, we examined (1) the trends in and status of marriage and labor force participation in American households, (2) how those trends have affected spousal benefits and retirement savings behavior within households today, and (3) the implications of these trends for future retirement security.

To address these questions, we analyzed several nationally-representative datasets, conducted an extensive literature review, and consulted with a wide range of experts. Specifically, to understand trends in family structure and work patterns, we analyzed data from the 1996 and 2008 panels of the Survey of Income and Program Participation (SIPP); the Integrated Public Use Microdata Series (IPUMS); and recent U.S. Census Bureau (Census) and Bureau of Labor Statistics (BLS) publications, which report on analyses of nationally-representative datasets such as the Current Population Survey (CPS). To determine the characteristics of the population receiving Social Security spousal benefits, we analyzed the 2008 restricted-use version of the SIPP data— known as the "Gold Standard" file—SIPP data that have been matched to administrative data on earnings and benefits from the Social Security Administration (SSA).[4]

To determine the characteristics of the population receiving spousal benefits through pensions, we used the 2010 version of the Survey of Consumer Finances (SCF), conducted by the Board of Governors of the Federal Reserve System (Federal Reserve). We also used the 2010 SCF to analyze retirement savings behavior among working-age households. To project the distribution of Social Security beneficiary types for women into the future, officials from the Office of Retirement Policy at SSA provided GAO with projections based on simulations they conducted with the Modeling Income in the Near Term model, Version 6 (MINT6). We conducted data reliability assessments of selected IPUMS, SIPP, SCF, and MINT6 data by conducting electronic data tests for completeness and accuracy, reviewing documentation on the dataset, or interviewing knowledgeable officials about how the data are collected and maintained and their appropriate uses. For the purposes of our analysis, we found the variables that we ultimately reported on to be sufficiently reliable.[5]

Lastly, to deepen our understanding of our data analyses and to understand the implications of demographic trends for retirement security, we conducted an extensive literature review and interviewed 49 experts from federal agencies, academia, advocacy groups, think tanks, and industry. We identified and interviewed experts who have specialized knowledge about spousal protections and retirement security in a specific area (e.g., law or social science), or who were recommended by one or more people or groups we had previously interviewed.[6]

We conducted this performance audit from September 2012 through January 2014 in accordance with generally accepted government auditing standards. Those standards require that we plan and perform the audit to obtain sufficient, appropriate evidence to provide a reasonable basis for our findings and conclusions based on our audit objectives. We believe that the evidence we obtained provides a reasonable basis for our findings and conclusions based on our audit objectives.

BACKGROUND

Financial Benefits of Marriage

A number of financial benefits associated with the institution of marriage relate to the ability of a couple to pool resources, specialize, and share risk. Specifically, married people can pool resources and share costs of household goods and services, which reduces the overall cost of items that do not need to be purchased individually and frees up resources for other types of investments. In addition, within married couples, even those in which both are working, each member can specialize in certain tasks, such as managing household finances. The financial benefits of marriage can carry over into retirement as couples continue to pool resources and assist each other as the risks of disability and deteriorating health increase.

Conversely, several factors contribute to the economic vulnerability of single retirees. First, single retirees living alone do not benefit from sharing the cost of living expenses and caregiving. According to the Census Bureau's poverty measures, a single person age 65 or older needs 79 percent of the income of a two-person household.[7] Moreover, unmarried individuals are more vulnerable to economic shocks, such as job loss, than their married counterparts. The unmarried, especially single parents, also tend to have fewer resources available to save for retirement during their working years. For example, a 2009 study shows that among all women age 35-54, never-married women with children had the lowest level of pension plan participation among all family types.[8] Taken together, these factors are likely to contribute to the higher poverty rates observed among unmarried individuals age 65 or older (see fig. 1).

Federal law also confers a number of benefits and protections for married spouses or former spouses.[9] In the case of certain types of retirement income, spouses or former spouses may receive retirement and survivor income based exclusively on marriage, independent of their own work history. This report focuses on four main sources of retirement income: (1) Social Security retirement benefits, (2) defined benefit (DB) plans, (3) defined contribution (DC) plans, and (4) individual retirement accounts (IRA).[10] Each of these is subject to different federal requirements and provides varying types and levels of protections to spouses of workers who are eligible for Social Security, participate in an employer sponsored DB or DC plan, or own an IRA. Examples of these requirements are summarized in table 1 and described in greater detail below.

Table 1. Selected Federal Requirements Related to Spousal Benefits or Protections in Social Security Retirement Benefits, Defined Benefit and Defined Contribution Plans, and Individual Retirement Accounts

	Marital Status at Retirement		
Source of Retirement Income	**Married**	**Widowed**	**Divorced**
Social Security Retirement Benefits	An eligible spouse is entitled to receive up to 50% of the retired worker's benefit, unless the spouse is entitled to a higher benefit based on his or her own work history.[a]	An eligible surviving spouse is entitled to receive up to 100% of the deceased worker's benefit, unless the survivor is entitled to a higher benefit based on his or her own work history.[a]	If the marriage lasted at least 10 years, an eligible divorced spouseis entitled to receive up to 50% of the divorced retired worker's benefit (a surviving divorced spouse is entitled to receive up to 100% of the deceased worker's benefit), unless the spouse is entitled to a retired worker benefit that is higher.[a, b]
Defined Benefit (DB) Plans	DB plans and some DC plans must provide benefits in the form of a qualified joint and survivor annuity (QJSA) or qualified preretirement survivor annuity (QPSA), meaning the spouse is entitled to receive annuity payments for his or her life should the participant spouse die either before or after retirement. The QJSA or QPSA may be waived only with the written consent of the spouse, witnessed by a plan representative or notary. For the QJSA, the survivor benefit must be at least half of the benefit payment the participant received during their joint lives.		Benefits provided to a former spouse will depend on the plan and the divorce settlement. A DB or DC plan may assign benefits toa spouse or former spouse pursuant to a divorce if the assignment is governed by a qualified domestic relations order (QDRO).
Defined Contribution (DC) Plans	DC plans that meet the following criteria are not required to offer QPSAs or QJSAs[c]: (1) the plan provides that 100% of the participant's vested account balance is to be paid to the surviving spouse upon the death of the participant; (2) the participant does not elect a life annuity; and (3) the participant's account does not include transfers from a plan subject to the standard QJSA/QPSA benefit rules (e.g., transfers from a money purchase or a DB plan).		

Table 1. (Continued)

	Marital Status at Retirement		
Source of Retirement Income	**Married**	**Widowed**	**Divorced**
	Written spousal consent is required to designate a non-spousal beneficiary. DC plans that meet these criteria may allow the employee, during his or her lifetime, to make withdrawals from the account or roll over the balance into an IRA without spousal consent.[d]		
Individual Retirement Accounts	There is no federal requirement to provide individual retirement account (IRA) benefits to a spouse unless he or she is a beneficiary. In general, an IRA owner may, during his or her lifetime, make withdrawals from the account without spousal consent.[d] Upon the death of the IRA owner, any remaining assets are to be distributed to the designated beneficiary(ies), if any. If there are none, assets will be distributed in accordance with the terms of the IRA documents and applicable state inheritance laws.[e]		Benefits provided to a former spouse will depend on the IRA documents and divorce settlement. An IRA owner may transfer IRA assets tax-free intoan IRA for a spouse or former spouse under a divorce instrument.[d]

Source: GAO analysis of applicable federal laws and regulations.

Notes: The specific benefits or protections a person may receive may vary depending on the individual circumstances, and additional requirements may apply that are not described here.

This table is limited to the following types of retirement income: Old-Age and Survivors Insurance benefits under the Social Security Act, DC and DB plans subject to regulation under the Employee Retirement Income Security Act and the Internal Revenue Code, and IRAs subject to requirements of the Internal Revenue Code.

[a] Other factors may affect the actual benefit amount. For example, actuarial reductions apply if workers/spouses claim benefits before full retirement age (which varies depending on the person's year of birth), with different size reductions for workers and spouses. Delayed retirement credits apply if they wait to collect benefits until after full retirement age.

[b] Special rules apply if a worker has been married more than once.

[c] Some DC plans, such as money purchase plans, are required to comply with the same requirements as DB plans (i.e., provide a QJSA or QPSA, and require the spouse's written consent to change this form of benefit).

[d] Pre-retirement withdrawals from DC plans and IRAs may be subject to tax penalties.

[e] Although the Internal Revenue Code provides for certain advantages for a spouse who is a designated beneficiary, the IRA owner is not required to designate his or her spouse as a beneficiary. There is also no federal requirement that an IRA owner

obtain spousal consent before designating a non-spouse beneficiary. However, in states with community property laws, the surviving spouse may be entitled to some of the IRA assets if he or she had not consented to the alternate beneficiary designation.

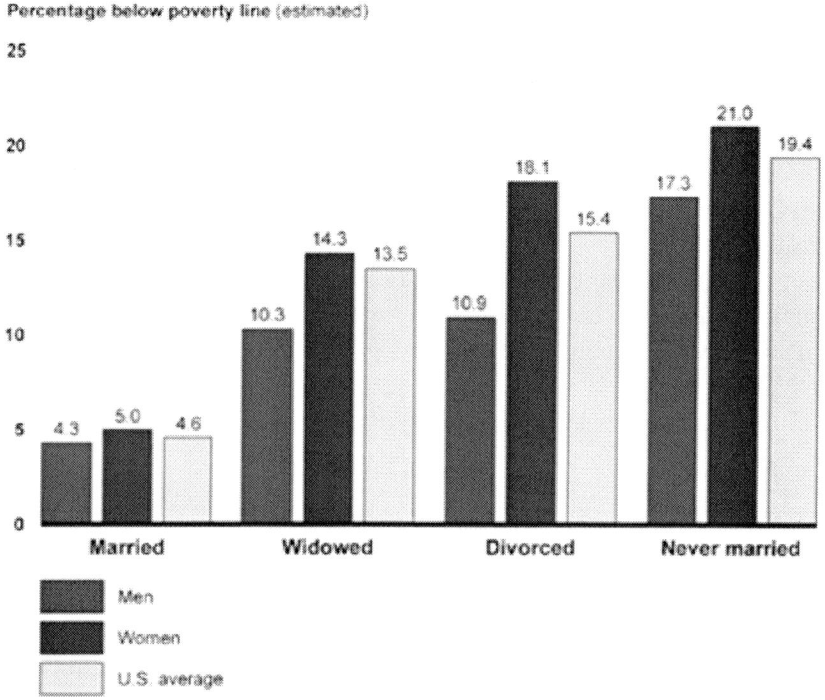

Source: GAO analysis of Current Population Survey data from the Census Bureau.
Note: All estimates in this figure have 95 percent confidence intervals within +/- 4.1 percentage points. Estimates of the poverty rates for married people have confidence intervals within +/- 0.6 percentage points.

Figure 1. Poverty Rate Estimates of the Population Age 65 and Older, by Marital Status and Sex, 2012.

Social Security

Social Security has been instrumental in reducing poverty among the elderly. From 1959 to 2007, the poverty rate for people age 65 and over decreased from about 35 percent to 9.7 percent, according to U.S. Census Bureau estimates. Experts have attributed much of this decline to the availability of Social Security benefits, which are also available to spouses and widows. Although Social Security is not meant to be the sole source of income for retirees, in 2011 nearly one-quarter of married beneficiaries and 45 percent of unmarried elderly beneficiaries age 65 and older relied on Social Security for at least 90 percent of their income, according to the Social Security Administration.

Table 2 below describes selected types of Social Security retirement benefits, eligibility criteria, and benefit levels for each type of benefit.[11] In this report, spousal benefits refer to both spouse-only and duallyentitled/spouse benefits. Survivor benefits refer to both widow(er)-only and dually-entitled/widow(er) benefits. Over the course of retirement, individuals can receive different types of Social Security retirement benefits. For example, an individual may receive retired-worker benefits while their spouse is alive (because their retired-worker benefit exceeds 50 percent of their spouse's benefit) but when the spouse dies, may receive a dually-entitled widow(er) benefit because their own retired-worker benefit does not exceed 100 percent of their spouse's benefit.[12]

Table 2. Selected Social Security Retirement Benefit Types and Characteristics

		Basis for Benefit		
Benefit Types	**Eligibility and Benefit Level**[a]	**Own work history**	**Spouse's work history**	**Has own qualifying work history, but benefit based on the spouse'swork history is higher**
Retired worker	A retired worker is eligible for benefits based on his or her work record and receives a benefit amount based on lifetime earnings, among other factors.	X		
Spouse-only	The spouse of a retired worker (including an eligible divorced spouse) is eligible to receive a benefit of up to 50% of the retired worker's benefit amount. Spouse-only beneficiaries do not qualify to receive benefits based on their own work record;		X	

		Basis for Benefit		
Benefit Types	**Eligibility and Benefit Level**[a]	**Own work history**	**Spouse's work history**	**Has own qualifying work history, but benefit based on the spouse'swork history is higher**
	for example, because they did not work at all or because they did not work long enough.			
Dually-entitled/spouse	A dually-entitled spouse (including an eligible divorced spouse) has a qualifying work history but receives a benefit based on the work records of his or her spouse because the spouse's benefit is higher. The benefit amount may be up to 50% of the retired worker's benefit amount.			X
Widow(er)-only	The widow(er) of a retired worker (including an eligible surviving divorced spouse) is eligible to receive a survivor benefit of up to 100% of the deceased retired worker's benefit amount. Widow(er)-only beneficiaries do not qualify to receive benefits based on their own work record; for example, because they did not work at all or because they did not work long enough.		X	
Dually-entitled/widow(er)	A dually-entitled widow(er) (including an eligible surviving divorced spouse) has a qualifying work history but receives a survivor benefit based on the work records			X

Table 2. (Continued)

		Basis for Benefit		
Benefit Types	**Eligibility and Benefit Level**[a]	**Own work history**	**Spouse's work history**	**Has own qualifying work history, but benefit based on the spouse'swork history is higher**
	of his or her spouse because the spouse's benefit is higher. The benefit amount may be up to 100% of the deceased retired worker's benefit amount.			

Source: GAO analysis of information provided by SSA and applicable federal laws and regulations.

Note: This table lists some of the benefits available under Social Security's Old-Age and Survivors Insurance program. For the purposes of this report, this table does not describe other Social Security program benefits, such as those based on a worker's disability or for dependent children. Divorced spouses and divorced survivors may qualify to receive all four types of spousal and survivor benefits based on a previous marriage to a retired worker if the marriage lasted at least 10 years. For a more comprehensive description of spouse and survivor benefits, see Alison M. Shelton and Dawn Nuschler, Congressional Research Service, *Social Security: Revisiting Benefits for Spouses and Survivors* (Washington, D.C.: Nov. 5, 2010).

[a] SSA uses a formula to calculate a retired worker's benefits, which typically takes into account the worker's highest 35 years of earnings, and adjusts or "indexes" each year of earnings to account for changes in average wages since the year the earnings were received. Other factors, such as the age of the worker and/or the spouse or widow(er), may affect the actual benefit amount for each beneficiary.

Defined Benefit Plans

DB plans typically offer benefits to a retiree in the form of an annuity that provides a monthly payment for life, the value of which is typically determined by a formula based on particular factors specified by the plan, such as salary and years of service. An annuity can help to protect a retiree against risks, including the risk of outliving one's assets (longevity risk) and, when an inflation-adjusted annuity is provided, the risk of inflation diminishing one's purchasing power. The Retirement Equity Act of 1984 required that DB plans provide benefits in the form of a qualified joint and survivor annuity (QJSA) or qualified preretirement survivor annuity (QPSA), unless waived by the worker and his or her spouse.[13] Some DB plans also give participants a choice to take lump-sum cash settlements, which could then be rolled over into an IRA, instead of taking a lifetime annuity.

Defined Contribution Plans

Under DC plans, workers and employers may make contributions to individual accounts. The most common type of DC plan is the 401(k) plan, which typically allows workers to contribute a portion of their pretax compensation to the plan, and may also provide for after-tax or employer contributions, depending on the plan. In contrast to DB plans, DC plan sponsors are generally not required to offer a lifetime annuity and most plans do not offer an annuity option, according to a study conducted for the Department of Labor.[14] Instead, at retirement, DC participants may take a lump sum or partial distribution, leave their money in the plan, roll their plan savings into an IRA, or purchase an annuity, depending on the options available under the plan.

Individual Retirement Accounts

Individual retirement accounts (IRAs), which may allow workers to receive favorable tax treatment for making contributions to an individual account,[15] and also generally accept rollover distributions from 401(k) and other retirement plans, are one of the fastest growing types of retirement assets in the United States, according to the Investment Company Institute, a national association of U.S. investment companies. As of the third quarter of 2013, IRA assets totaled approximately $6 trillion, accounting for 28 percent of U.S. retirement assets, according to the Investment Company Institute.

Same-Sex Marriages

In 2013, same-sex spouses became eligible for a number of federal benefits for the first time since the first state allowed same-sex marriages in 2004. In June 2013, the U.S. Supreme Court struck down a provision of the Defense of Marriage Act (DOMA), which had established an opposite-sex definition of "marriage" and "spouse" for any act of Congress or any ruling, regulation, or interpretation by federal bureaus and agencies.[16] As a result of DOMA, enacted in 1996, same-sex couples married under state law were not covered by some of the federal requirements described above; for example, sponsors of private-sector pensions regulated by ERISA were not required to offer survivor benefits to same-sex spouses. At the time of this report's issuance, the Executive Branch had issued some guidance and was in the process of determining what additional guidance to issue, or other actions to take, in response to the U.S. Supreme Court ruling.[17]

State of the U.S. Retirement System and Economy

Today, working-age households face a host of challenges in saving for retirement. First, less than half (46 percent) of all workers age 16 and older participated in some form of employment-based pension plan in 2012,[18] raising concerns about the adequacy of retirement savings among future retirees. Second, employers have been moving from DB to DC plans. Further, many of the remaining DB plans now offer lump sums as one of the form-of-payment options under the plan;[19] participants who elect a lump sum do so in lieu of a lifetime annuity. Some DB plan sponsors have also begun offering special, one-time lump sum elections to participants who are already retired and receiving monthly pension benefits;[20] participants who accept such offers give up their lifetime annuity. As a result of all of these trends and actions, those who do participate in an employer-sponsored plan have increasing responsibility to manage their pensions and other financial assets so that they have a sufficiently adequate income throughout retirement. However, recent research suggests that as life expectancy continues to increase, many Americans—including baby boomers, who are beginning to retire in greater numbers—may outlive their retirement assets.

The trends in the U.S. economy overall have exacerbated the challenges households face in saving for retirement. The 2007-2009 recession resulted in major stock indices falling dramatically, reducing retirement savings at a critical time for those in or near retirement. Further, the recession led to higher rates of unemployment among older workers. Prior GAO work has shown that long-term unemployment can reduce an older worker's future retirement income in numerous ways, including reducing the number of years the worker can accumulate savings, prompting workers to claim Social Security retirement benefits early, and leading workers to draw down retirement savings to pay for living expenses during unemployment.[21]

THE COMPOSITION AND WORK PATTERNS OF THE FAMILY HAVE CHANGED DRAMATICALLY IN THE PAST 50 YEARS

As Marriage Has Declined, Cohabitation and Single Parenthood Have Increased

Since 1960, marriage rates in the United States have been declining. From 1960 through 2010, the proportion of the population age 15 and above that is married declined from 68 to 54 percent (see fig. 2). Over the same period, the proportion of divorced individuals increased from 2 to 10 percent, and the proportion of individuals who were never married climbed from 22 to 31 percent.[22] These statistics represent a snapshot at a particular point in time. Therefore, those who were unmarried at one point in time might marry at a later point in time and vice versa. One reason for the rising proportion of the never-married is that many people have begun getting married later in life. According to the Census Bureau, from 1960 through 2011, the median age of first marriage increased from an estimated 20 to 27 for women and 23 to 29 for men.

Over the past two decades it has also become more common for single people to live together before they get married. Specifically, between 1995 and 2006-2010, the percentage of women who cohabited as a first union increased from 34 to 48 percent, according to a study by the Department of Health and Human Services.[23] Overall, the number of unmarried cohabiting couples climbed from 2.9 to 7.8 million from 1996 through 2012, according to CPS estimates (see fig. 3). A significant proportion of these households have children under 18 years old. These households do not include same-sex partnerships. Due to limitations in the way these data are collected, both the number of same-sex cohabitating couples and same-sex married couples are unclear.[24]

Along with the increase in unmarried couples with children over the last several decades, the percentage of single-parent families rose. In fact, according to CPS estimates, from 1970 through 2012, the proportion of single-parent families more than doubled, increasing from 13 to 32 percent of all families. The vast majority of single-parent households were headed by women (see fig. 4).

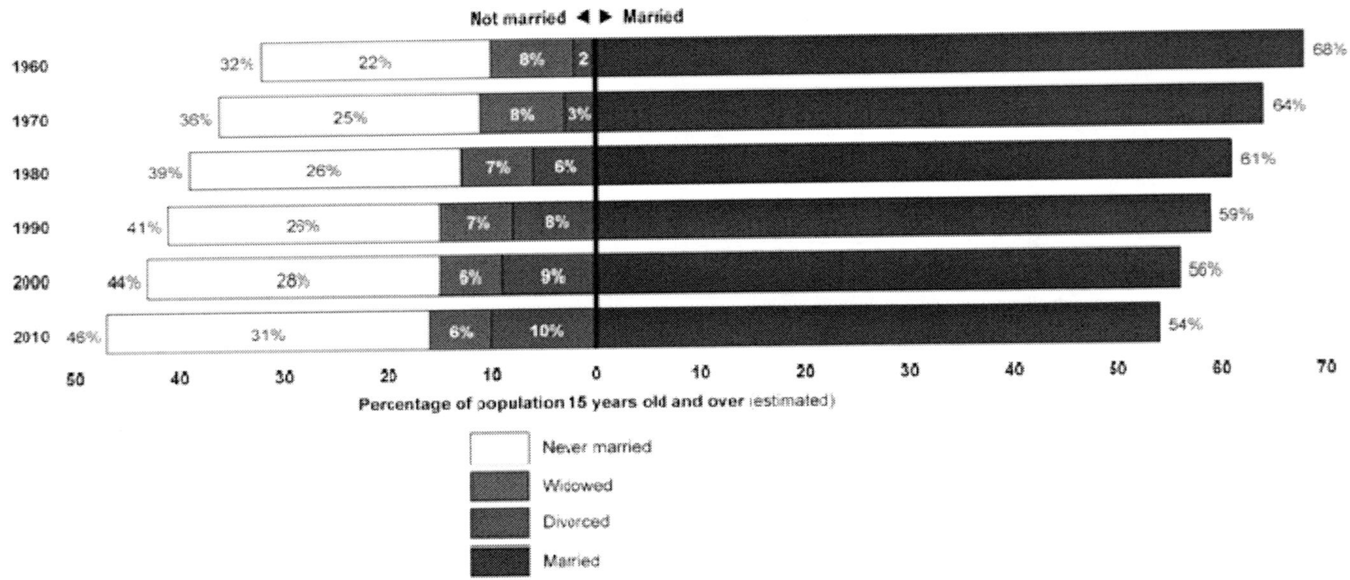

Source: GAO analysis of CPS data.

Note: All estimates in this figure have margins of error at the 95% confidence level that are less than or equal to 0.6 percentage points. These statistics represent a snap shot at a particular point in time. Therefore, those who were unmarried at one point in time might become married at a later point in time and vice versa. Percentages within the not married sub-categories may not sum to the not married total due to rounding.

Figure 2. Estimated Percentage of Population Age 15 and Older by Marital Status: 1960-2010.

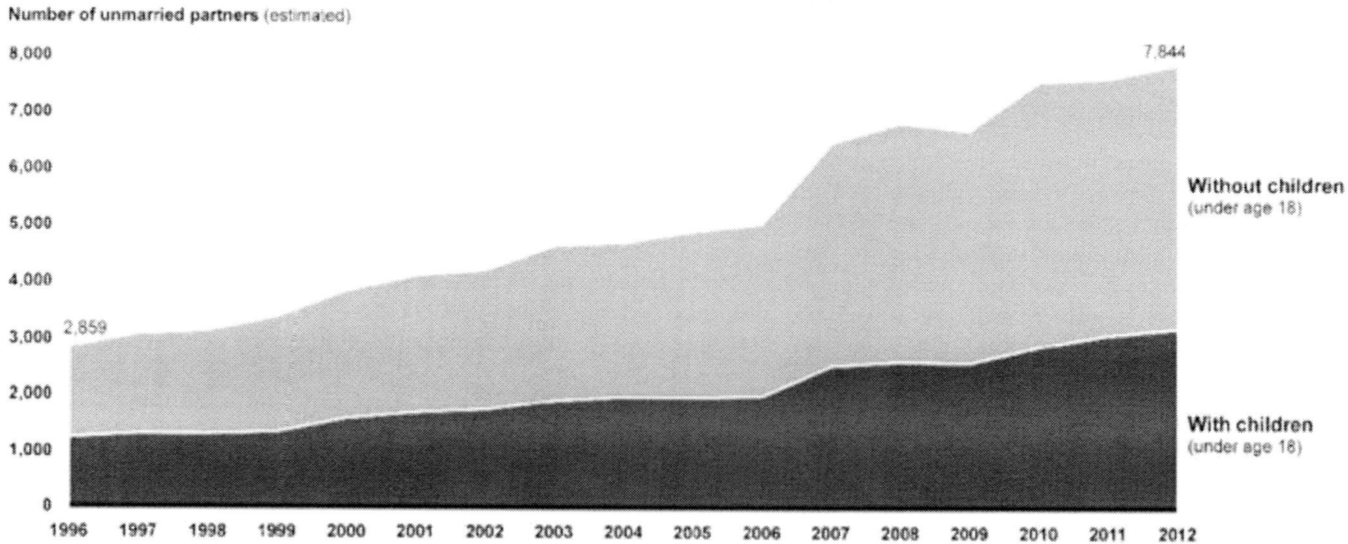

Source: Current Population Survey.

Note: All estimates in this figure have margins of error at the 95% confidence level that are less than or equal to 300,000. It should be noted that the jump between 2006 and 2007 occurred because of a change in measurement: in 2007, the Census Bureau began asking a direct question in the CPS Annual Social and Economic Supplement about the presence of unmarried partners. According to Census Bureau analyses, the increase between 2009 and 2010 appears to reflect a true increase.

Figure 3. Estimated Number of Unmarried Couples (in Thousands): 1996-2012.

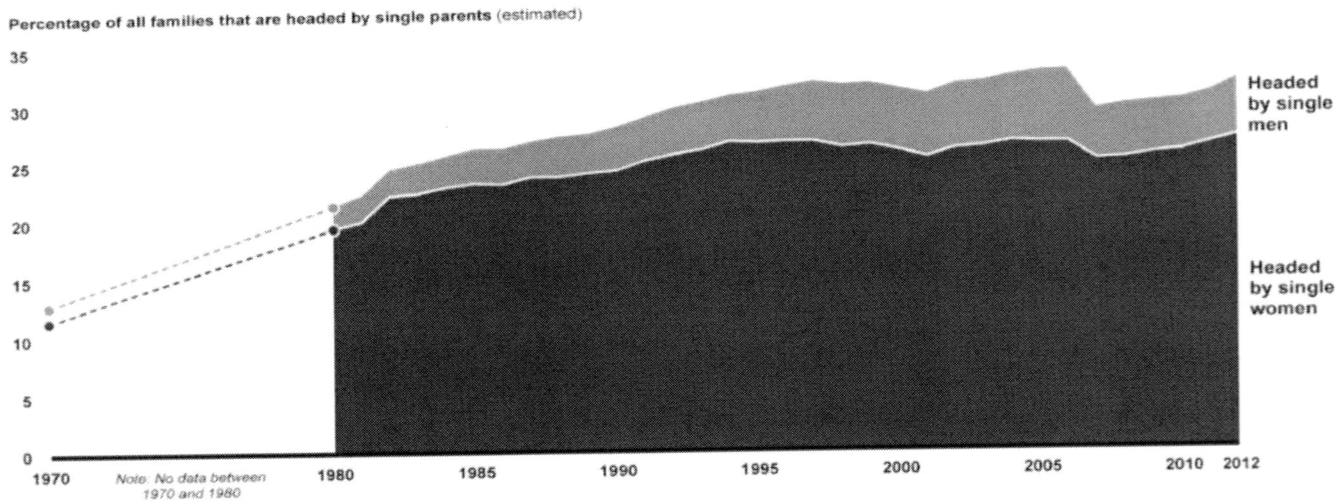

Source: GAO analysis of Current Population Survey data.

Note: All estimates in this figure have margins of error at the 95% confidence level that are less than or equal to 0.4 percentage points. Note that the drop seen in 2007 occurs because of measurement changes in the CPS Annual Social and Economic Supplement. Prior to 2007, the data show all unmarried parents. Specifically, the data prior to 2007 include both unmarried parents who are cohabiting with the parent of at least one of their children, and "lone parents"—unmarried parents who are not cohabiting with the parent of any of their children. Starting in 2007, the data identify unmarried parents who are cohabiting with the parent of at least one of their children. These cohabiting parents were excluded from the data, so only lone parent families are shown in the chart starting in 2007.

Figure 4. Among All Families, Estimated Percentage of Single-Parent Families by Sex of Head of Household: 1970-2012.

The Decline in Marriage Is More Pronounced for Certain Demographic Groups

The decline in marriage has been more pronounced for certain racial and ethnic groups as well as income and education levels.[25] Among racial and ethnic groups, blacks have experienced the greatest decline in marriage (see fig. 5). From 1960 through 2010, the percentage of married black men fell from 61 to 39 and the percentage of married black women fell from 60 to 33. Differences in marriage rates between blacks and other racial and ethnic categories persisted even after accounting for differences in income and education levels, and controlling for age.[26]

Asians were the only group, among these racial and ethnic groups, to experience an uptick in marriage since 2000.

Since the 1970s, the percentage of single-parent families has increased dramatically (see fig. 6). Specifically, from 1970 through 2012 (and from 1980 through 2012 in the case of Hispanics), the percentage of single-parent families climbed for every race and ethnicity category depicted in the figure, with the highest growth among whites (an increase of 17 percentage points, for a 170 percent increase in the percentage). However, over the entire period, the rate of single parenthood was highest among black families and continues to be more than double the rate of white families.

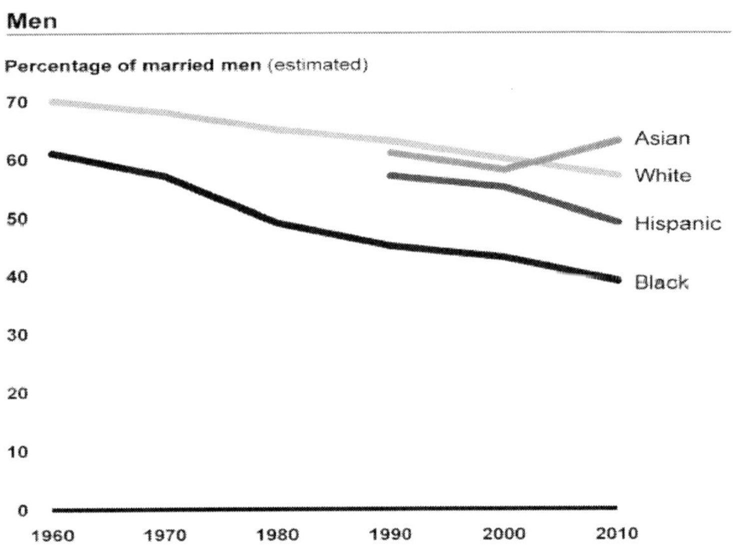

Figure 5. (Continued).

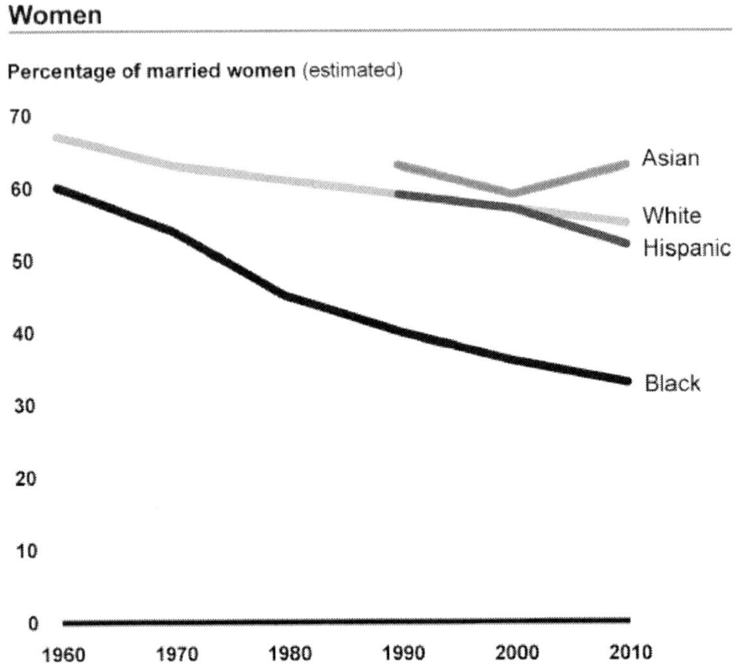

Source: GAO analysis of CPS data.

Note: Individuals in the white, black, and Asian race categories may be Hispanic. Prior to 2003, individuals in the Current Population Survey were required to select only one race. Beginning in 2003, individuals were allowed to select multiple race groups. Starting in 2003, the race categories in this chart include only people who reported only a single race group. Percentage estimates in this figure have margins of error at the 95% confidence level that are less than or equal to 0.6 percentage points for whites; 2.4 percentage points for blacks; 4 percentage points for Asians; and 2.2 percentage points for Hispanics.

Figure 5. Estimated Percentage of Married Individuals by Race and Gender over Time: 1960-2010.

The decline in marriage and rise in single parenthood over this period were also more pronounced among low-income and less-educated populations. Over the period from 1960 through 2010 the percentage of married, 45- to 54-year-olds in the highest income quintile declined slightly for men (see fig. 7). In contrast, over the same period, the percentage of married, 45- to 54-year-old men and women in the lowest income quintile declined markedly.

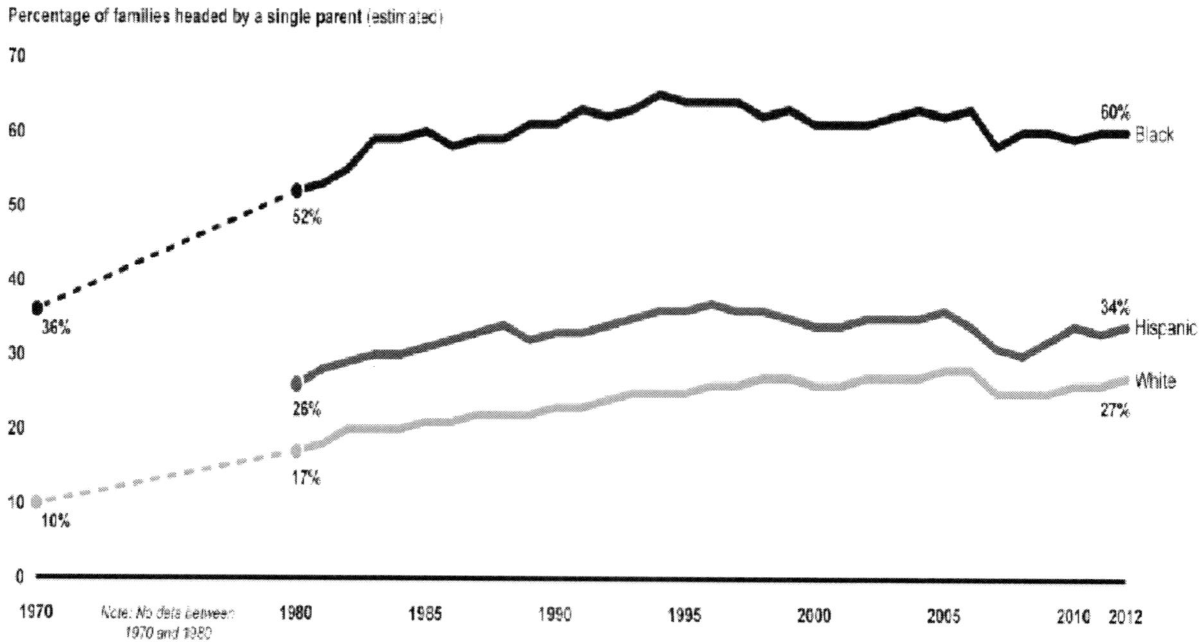

Source: GAO analysis of Current Population Survey data.

Note: Individuals in the white and black race categories may be Hispanic. Prior to 2003, individuals in the Current Population Survey were required to select only one race. Beginning in 2003, individuals were allowed to select multiple race groups. Starting in 2003, the race categories in this chart include only people who reported only a single race group. Percentage estimates in this figure have margins of error at the 95% confidence level that are less than or equal to 1.8 percentage points. Note that the drop seen in 2007 occurs because of measurement changes in the CPS Annual Social and Economic Supplement.

Specifically, the data prior to 2007 include both unmarried parents who are cohabiting with the parent of at least one of their children, and "lone parents"—unmarried parents who are not cohabiting with the parent of any of their children. Starting in 2007, the data identify unmarried parents who are cohabiting with the parent of at least one of their children. These cohabiting parents were excluded from the data, so only lone parent families are shown in the chart starting in 2007.

Figure 6. Estimated Percentage of Families Headed by a Single Parent by Race: 1970-2012.

Similarly, the percentage of single parents among 45- to 54-year-old men and women in the highest income quintile remained flat, while there was a steep rise in the percentage of single parents in the lowest income quintile during this timeframe.

For education, among individuals age 18 years and older, the decline in the percentage of married individuals was steeper for those with less than a high school diploma than for those with 4 or more years of college. Conversely, the rise in single parenthood was steeper for women and men without a high school diploma in comparison to their counterparts with 4 or more years of college (see fig. 8).

Nonetheless, the rate of single parenthood among college-educated women was greater than that of men with less than a high school diploma for most of the period, reflecting the higher rate of single parenthood among women overall.

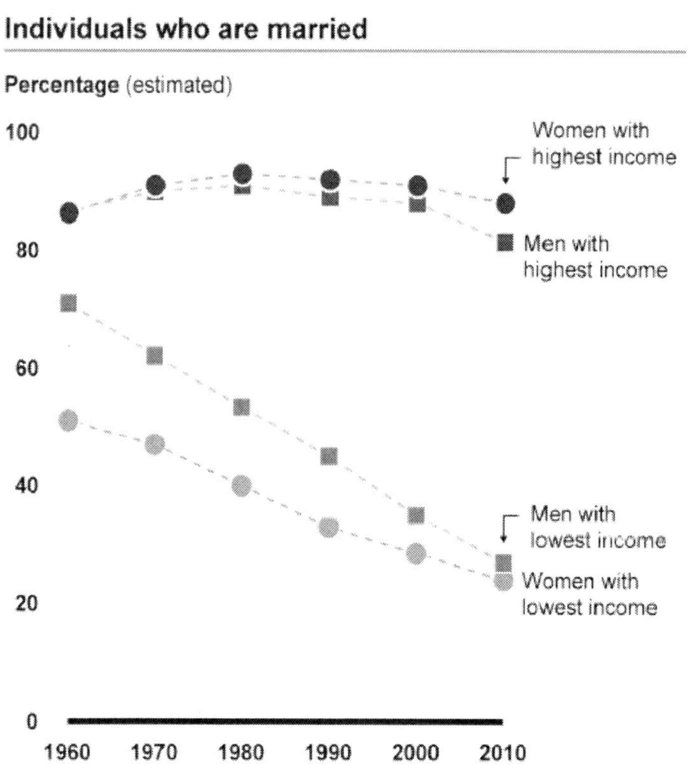

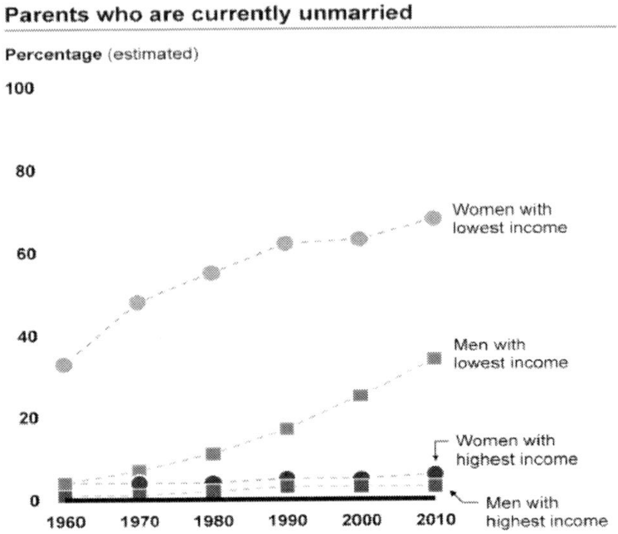

Source: GAO analysis of IPUMS data.

Note: Percentage estimates in this figure have margins of error at the 95% confidence level that are less than or equal to 1.7 percentage points. "Parents who are currently unmarried" refers to adults with their own children in the home and whose current marital status is divorced, separated, widowed, or never married.

Figure 7. Among People Age 45-54, Estimated Percentage of Married Men and Women, and Unmarried Parents, by Highest and Lowest Income Quintiles: 1960-2010.

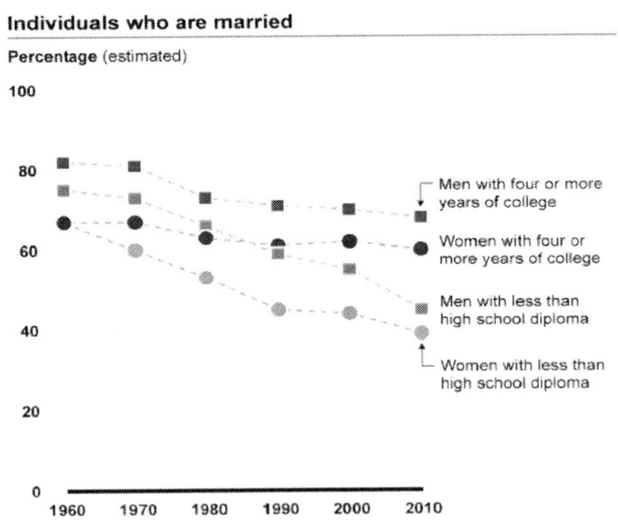

Figure 8. (Continued)

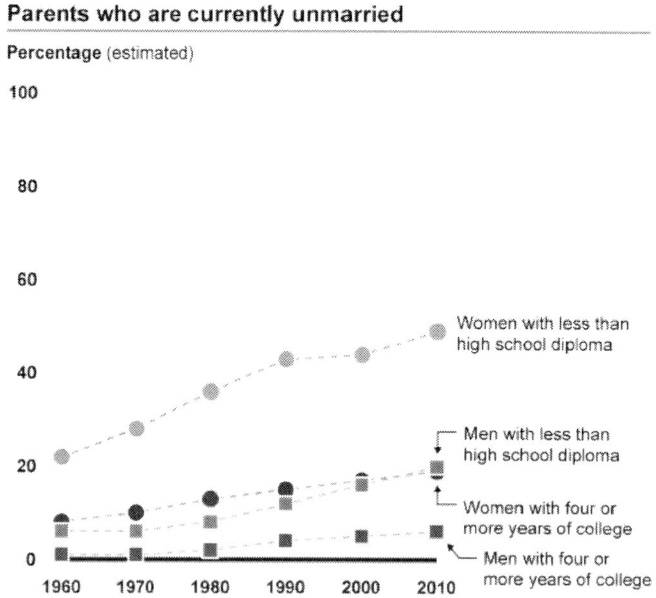

Source: GAO analysis of IPUMS data.

Note: Percentage estimates in this figure have margins of error at the 95% confidence level that are less than or equal to 1.3 percentage points. "Parents who are currently unmarried" here refers to any adult with their own children in the home whose current marital status is divorced, separated, widowed, or never married.

Figure 8. Among People Age 18 and Older, Estimated Percentage of Married Men and Women, and Unmarried Parents, by Education Level: 1960-2010.

Married Women Are Participating in the Labor Force at Higher Rates and Are Taking Less Time Off for Caregiving

Labor force participation among married and single men and women changed substantially over the past 50 years (see fig. 9). In 1960, labor force participation rates among the four groups (married men, single men, married women, and single women) ranged from 89 percent for married men to 32 percent for married women. The variation in workforce participation rates between single men (70 percent) and single women (59 percent) was not as wide, but was still substantial. Since then, the differences in labor force participation rates for these four groups have narrowed. In 2010, the rate was 76 percent for married men, 67 percent for single men, 63 percent for single women, and 61 percent for married women. However, as figure 9 shows, the labor force participation rates of married women have leveled off since the mid-nineties, and have declined for single women, single men, and married men over the last decade.[27]

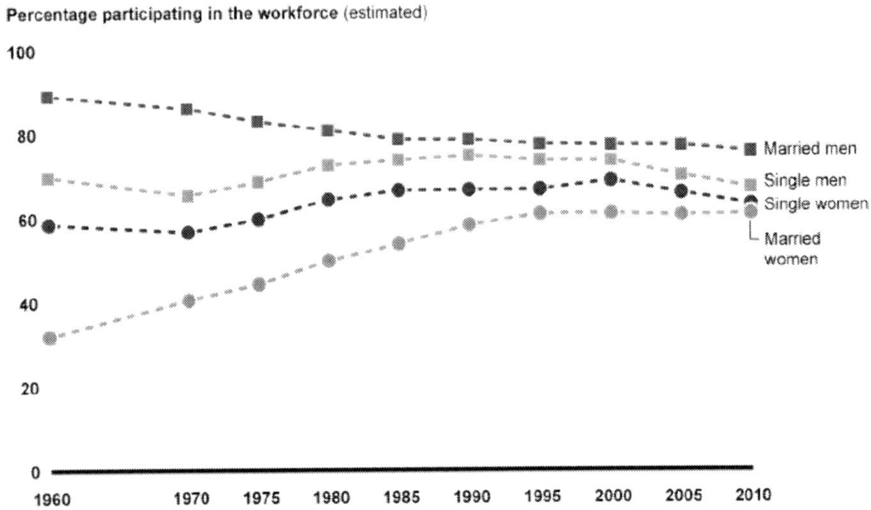

Source: Current Population Survey.

Note: Percentage estimates in this figure have margins of error at the 95% confidence level that are less than or equal to 1.2 percentage points. The categories for single men and single women include all unmarried people, including those who are divorced, widowed, or who were never married.

Figure 9. Estimated Labor Force Participation Rates by Sex and Marital Status: 1960-2010.

Labor force participation rates for women with children followed a similar trajectory to those of married women. From 1975 through 2010, labor force participation rates for women with children under age 3 grew from 34 to 61 percent (see fig. 10).[28] For women with children under age 6, the rate grew from 39 to 64 percent. As in the case of married women, labor force participation rates for each of these groups have remained relatively level since the mid-1990s.[29]

As a result of married women's increasing labor force participation, the proportion of married couples with two earners has risen—along with the wives' contributions to household income.

The proportion of households in which both the husband and wife contributed to their household's income rose from 44 percent in 1967 to 60 percent in 1994 (see fig. 11).

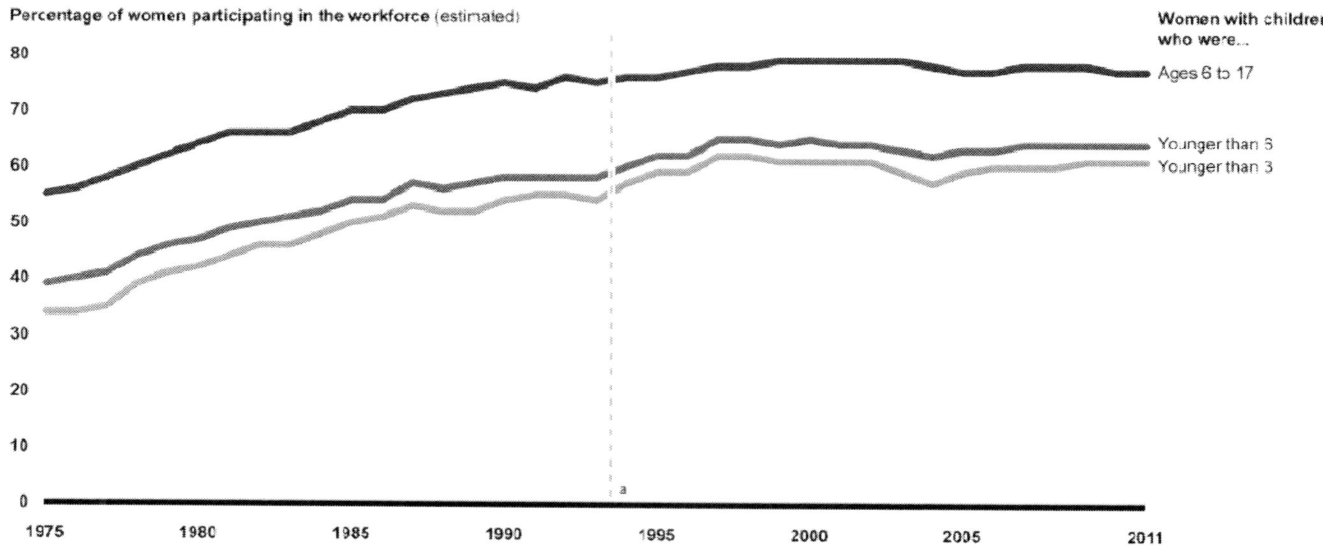

Source: Annual Social and Economic Supplements, Current Population Survey.

Note: Children are "own" children and include sons, daughters, stepchildren, and adopted children. Not included are nieces, nephews, grandchildren, and other related and unrelated children. Percentage estimates in this figure have margins of error at the 95% confidence level that are less than or equal to 1.8 percentage points.

[a]Data for 1994 and subsequent years are not directly comparable with data for 1993 and earlier because of the introduction of a major redesign of the Current Population Survey.

Figure 10. Estimated Labor Force Participation Rates among Women with Children of Different Ages: 1975-2010.

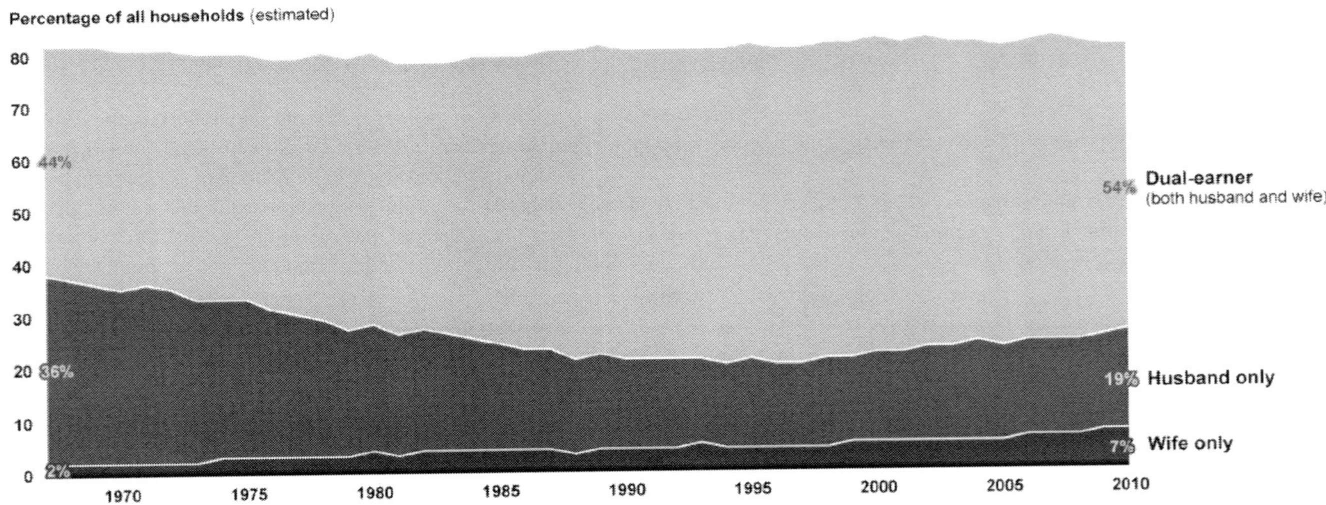

Source: Current Population Survey data, Annual Social and Economic Supplements.

Note: Married households in which neither spouse works and married households in which additional earners contribute to family income are not depicted in this figure, and comprise the remainder of the 100 percent of all married households. Percentage estimates in this figure have margins of error at the 95% confidence level that are less than or equal to 0.5 percentage points.

Figure 11. Among Married Households, Estimated Percentage of Married Households in Which Both Husband and Wife Have Earnings, Only the Husband Has Earnings, and Only the Wife Has Earnings: 1967-2010.

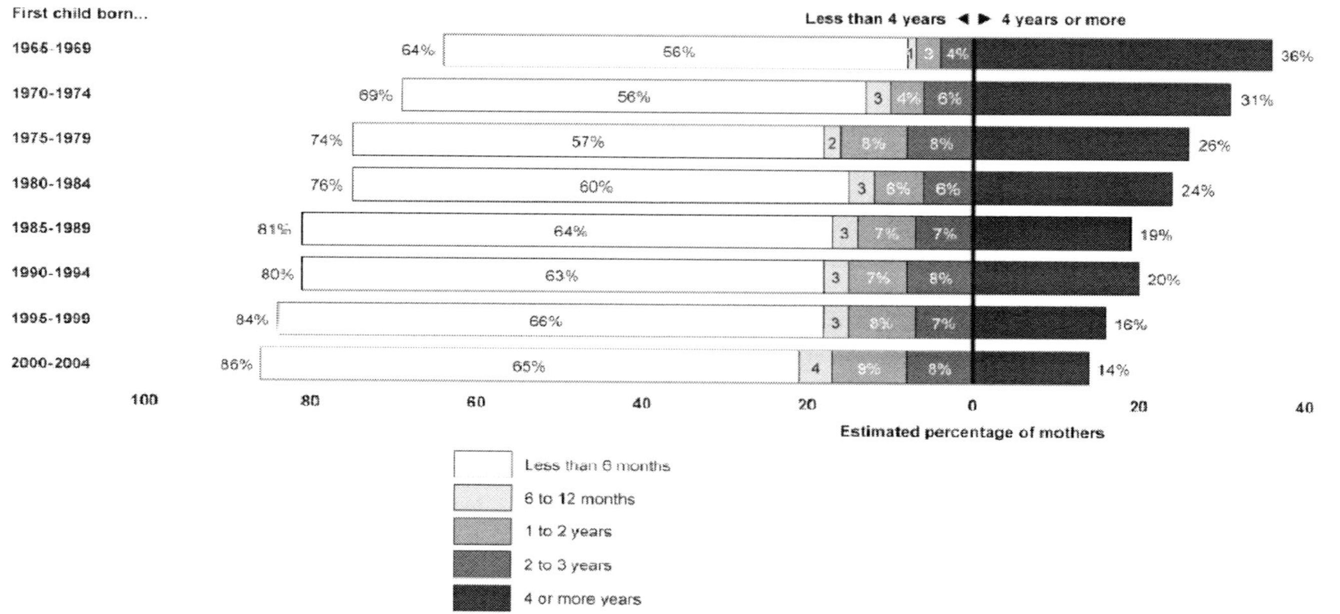

Source: GAO analysis of 2008 SIPP data.

Note: Percentages within the "less than 4 years" category may not sum to the "less than 4 years" total due to rounding. This figure comprises mothers age 20 through 62 who worked prior to the birth of their first child. The employment history data were collected in Wave 1 of the 2008 SIPP, which took place in 2008. There is some potential overlap between the categories of spell length exceeding 6 months. The SIPP data precisely identify women in the category "Less than 6 months." However, there is less precision in the other categories.

This is because if a woman reports that she has taken off 6 months or more, she is asked to provide the start and end date for each spell out of the workforce; however, the SIPP data only provide the start and end year of each spell, so we do not know the month in which each spell started and ended. Therefore, there is potential for overlap in the categories of timeframes. For example, a woman whose spell started in January 2000 and ended in February 2001 – a 13-month spell – would be grouped in the "1-2 years" category. But a woman whose spell started in December 2000 and ended in January 2002 – also a 13-month spell – would be grouped in the "2-3 years" category. Margins of error at the 95% confidence level for estimates of the percent of women taking off less than 6 months are less than or equal to 5.6 percentage points, for each bar. Margins of error for estimates of the percent of women taking off 4 or more years are less than or equal to 4.8 percentage points, for each bar. Margins of error for estimates of the percent of women taking off periods between 6 months and 3 years range from 0.4 to 2.0 percentage points. Note that these estimates are less reliable—the standard errors can be as high as 30 percent of the estimates for the earliest childbirth cohort, although they are always less than 15 percent of the estimates for estimates from 1980 and later. For women who had their first child between 2005 and 2007, 73 percent took less than 6 months off from work. For these women, we could not report on longer periods of time out of the workforce because insufficient time had passed between when their first child was born and when the data were collected.

Figure 12. Among Mothers Who Worked prior to the Birth of Their First Child, Length of Time off Taken for Caregiving, by Year First Child Was Born.

The proportion remained at 60 percent through 2000, after which it declined to 54 percent by 2010. Part of this is likely explained by the stagnation in married women's labor force participation rates over that period, but part of this also may be due to the rise in the percentage of married households in which only the wife works.

Since 1967, the proportion of married households in which the wife was the sole earner rose more than threefold—from 2 to 7 percent.

At the same time, the proportion of married households in which the husband was the sole earner declined from 36 to 19 percent. Women's contributions to family income also grew steadily over this period.

According to the Bureau of Labor Statistics, from 1970 through 2010, women's median contribution to household income rose from 27 to 38 percent. Further, from 1987 through 2010, the percentage of households in which the wives' earnings exceeded their husband's rose from 24 to 38 percent.[30]

As working women's contributions to household income have grown, women have also tended to take less time out of the workforce to raise children.

Since the 1960s, working women have left the workforce for progressively shorter intervals to care for their first born children. For children born in the late 1960s, 36 percent of working mothers took 4 years or more off to care for their first born and 56 percent took less than 6 months off (see fig. 12).

For children born from 2000 through 2004, 14 percent of working women took 4 years or more off and 65 percent took less than 6 months off.[31]

It is also noteworthy that the women represented in figure 12—those who were working prior to the birth of their first child—comprised a growing proportion of new mothers over this period, according to analysis by the Census Bureau.

Specifically, an estimated 60 percent of women who had their first child between 1960 and 1965 had worked for at least 6 months or more continuously prior to having children.

In contrast, an estimated 75 percent of women who had their first child between 2000 and 2005 had worked for 6 or more months continuously prior to childbirth.[32]

Trends in Marriage and Work Patterns Have Resulted in Fewer Women Receiving Social Security Spousal Benefits and Married Women Contributing More to Household Savings

Fewer Women Are Receiving Social Security Spousal Benefits

Fewer women are receiving Social Security spousal benefits today than in the past.[33] In 1960, nearly one-third of all women over age 62 received spousal benefits based exclusively on their spouse's work record, according to SSA data (see fig. 13). In 2011, 9 percent of women received them. Similarly, the proportion of women over age 62 receiving widow (i.e., survivor) benefits based exclusively on their spouse's work record declined from 23 to 16 percent over the same period. At the same time, as women's workforce participation and earnings have risen, the percentage of women receiving benefits based solely on their own work record increased from about 39 to 48 percent. However, women's average Social Security retired worker benefit is approximately three-quarters of men's average retired worker benefit due to women's lower median lifetime earnings relative to men's. Specifically, according to SSA, in 2012, the average retired worker benefit was $1,417 per month for men and $1,103 per month for women.

In addition to the effect of rising labor force participation, the decline in women's receipt of spousal benefits is partly due to the decline in marriage. Specifically, the proportion of women who are not eligible to receive Social Security spousal benefits because they were either never married, or divorced after less than 10 years of marriage—the length of time required for eligibility for Social Security divorced spouse benefits— has increased over the last two decades. According to analysis by SSA researchers, among women age 50-59, the percentage who were not eligible to receive Social Security spouse or widow benefits based on marital history doubled from 8 to 16 percent from 1990 to 2009 (see fig. 14).[34] However, this growth varied greatly by race. For blacks, the rise in ineligibility for spousal or widow benefits has been more dramatic, growing from 13 to 34 percent from 1990 to 2009.[35] In contrast, among whites and Hispanics, the rates of ineligibility grew less—by 8 and 6 percentage points, respectively.

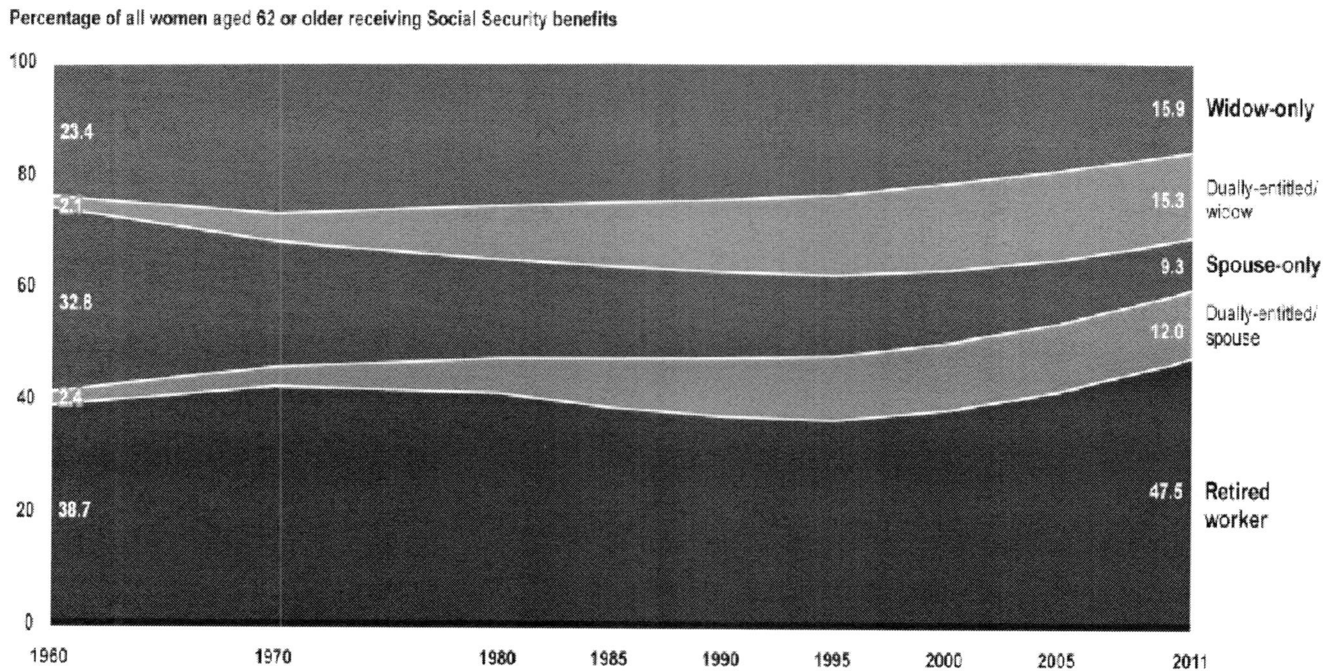

Source: Annual Statistical Supplement to the Social Security Bulletin, 2012.

Figure 13. Percentage of All Women Age 62 or Older by Social Security Benefit Status over Time.

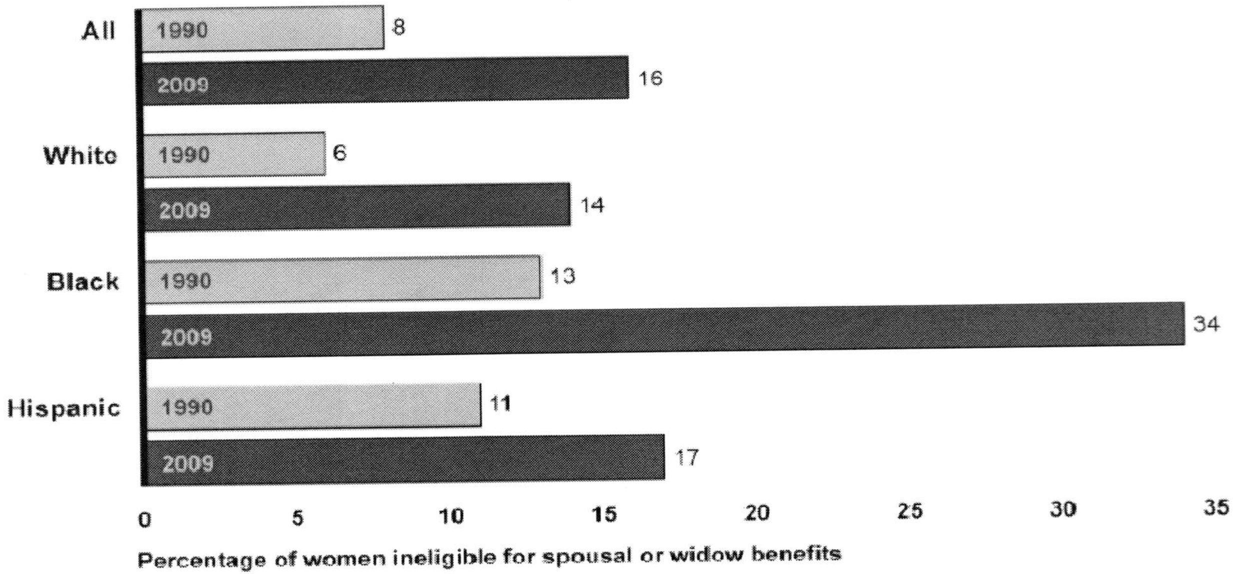

Source: Howard M. Iams and Christopher R. Tamborini, "The Implications of Marital History Change on Woman's Eligibility for Social Security Wife and Widow Benefits, 1990-2009," Social Security Bulletin, vol. 72, no. 2 (2012).

Note: In this figure, women ineligible for Social Security spouse or widow benefits because of marital history include women who were never married or who were divorced without any 10-year marriage at the time of the survey. For each category above, the difference between the proportion of women ineligible for Social Security spouse or widow benefits because of marital history in 1990 and 2009 was statistically significant at the 0.05 level.

Figure 14. Estimated Percentage of Women Ineligible for Social Security Spouse or Widow Benefits Because of Marital History among 50-59 Year Olds by Race: 1990 and 2009.

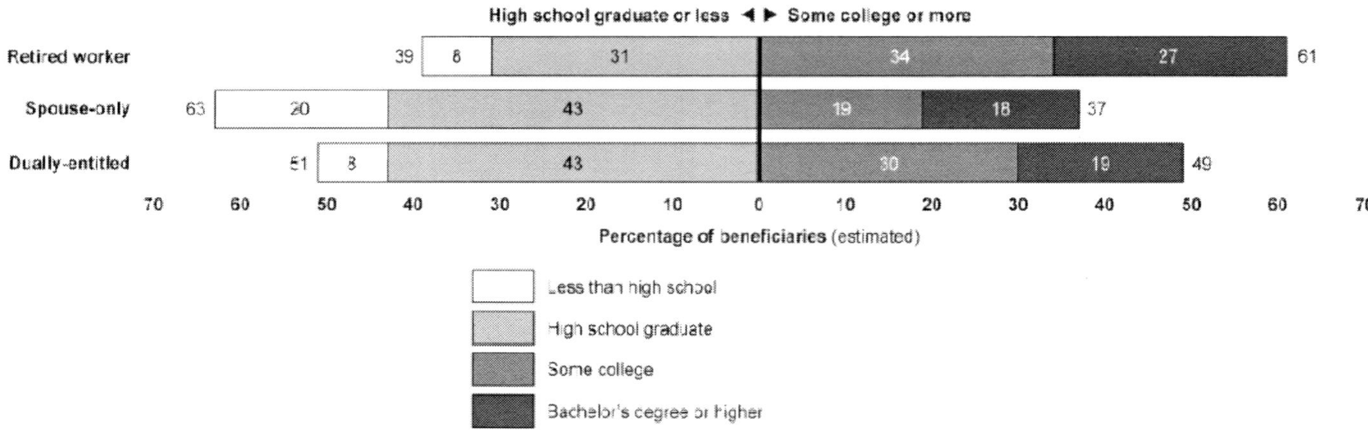

Source: GAO analysis of SIPP Gold Standard data.

Note: Widows were excluded from the sample of retired workers so that we could compare a similar set of female beneficiaries (i.e., all non-widows).

Figure 15. Education Levels of Women Receiving Social Security Benefits Based on Their Own Work Record (Retired Worker), Their Spouse's Work Record (Spouse-only) or Both (Dually-entitled/Spouse): 2011.

The growth in ineligibility also varied by income, and the differences in eligibility rates by income grew over time, according to our analysis of SIPP data.[36] Within the lowest income quintile, from 1996 to 2008, the percentage of 50-59 year-old women who were married or had been married for at least 10 years declined from an estimated 78 to 65 percent. In contrast, among women in the same age range, but in the highest income quintile, the percentage who were married or had been married for at least 10 years declined from an estimated 97 to 94 percent.[37,38]

Today's female spouse-only beneficiaries differ from female beneficiaries with a qualifying work record in terms of race, education, and family size, but not in terms of their wealth. Spouse-only beneficiaries are less likely to be black than women receiving benefits based exclusively on their own work record (retired worker beneficiaries). Dually-entitled beneficiaries, in contrast, are more likely to be white than their counterparts receiving retired worker or spousal benefits. Spouse-only beneficiaries are also less likely to be college educated (see fig. 15). In fact, 63 percent of spouse-only beneficiaries have less than a college education. At the same time, 39 and 51 percent of retired worker and dually-entitled beneficiaries have less than a college education, respectively.

Among married women, spouse-only beneficiaries have significantly more children (an average of 3.1 vs. 2.4 and 2.8 among retired-worker and dually-entitled beneficiaries, respectively). In terms of earnings and wealth, married spouse-only beneficiaries have lower lifetime household earnings than their married counterparts who receive retired-worker benefits or are dually-entitled, but have comparable levels of total net worth, home ownership, and home equity.[39]

Married Women's Contributions to Household Account-Based Retirement Savings Approach Men's in Dual-Earner Households

With women's rising workforce participation and earnings, married women are contributing more to household account-based retirement savings, but their share of contributions varies with the work patterns of the household. Between 1992 and 2010, married women's contributions to household account-based retirement savings (accumulated in DC plans, IRAs, and Keoghs) increased from 20 to 38 percent, on average, according to our analysis of SCF data.[40] However, the proportion of households with any retirement savings and the average proportion of the wives' contributions varied depending on whether the husband, wife, or both were working.

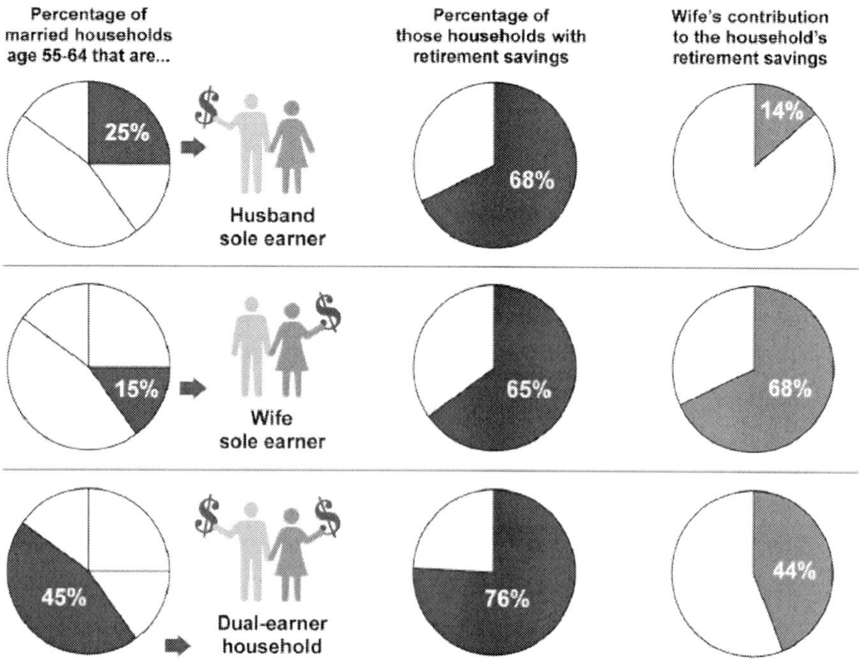

Source: GAO analysis of 2010 Survey of Consumer Finances data.

Note: Married households in which neither spouse works are not depicted in this figure (and comprise the remainder of the 100 percent of all married households). All estimates in this figure have 95 percent confidence intervals within +/- 8.1 percentage points of the estimates themselves. Household retirement savings include the balance of all defined contribution, IRA (Roth, traditional, and rollover), and Keogh accounts held by all members of the primary economic unit, as defined by the Survey of Consumer Finances. DB plans are not included in this measure of household savings.

Figure 16. Among Married Households Age 55-64 Years Old, Average Proportion of Household Retirement Savings (Defined Contribution Plans and Individual Retirement Accounts) Contributed by Each Spouse: 2010.

In 2010, dual-earner households were the most common type of households among 55- to 64-year-olds, comprising 45 percent of married households for that age group that year (see fig. 16). These households were more likely to have account-based retirement savings than households with only one spouse working. Further, among dual-earner households with account-based retirement savings (either in DC plans, IRAs, our Keoghs), wives contributed 44 percent of the household's account-based retirement savings, on average.[41] For households with some account-based retirement savings in which wives were the sole earners, wives contributed 68 percent of the household's account-based retirement savings. In contrast, wives contributed much lower shares of retirement savings—14 percent, on average—in households in which the husband was the sole earner.[42]

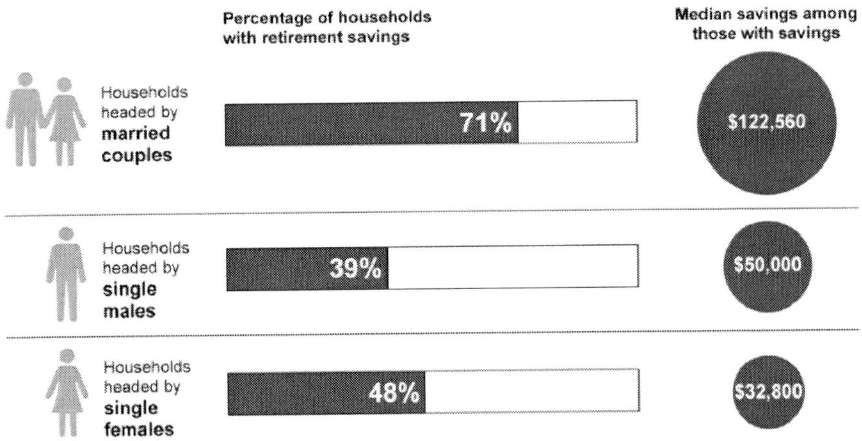

Source: GAO analysis of 2010 Survey of Consumer Finances data.

Note: Median savings are expressed in 2010 dollars. All percentage estimates in this figure have 95 percent confidence intervals within +/- 4.8 percentage points of the estimate itself. All median dollar estimates in this figure have 95 percent confidence intervals within +/- 13,071 dollars of the estimate itself. Household retirement savings include the balance of all defined contribution, IRA (Roth, traditional, and rollover), and Keogh accounts held by all members of the primary economic unit, as defined by the Survey of Consumer Finances. DB plans are not included in this measure of household savings.

Figure 17. Among All Households Age 50-64, Percentage of Households with Retirement Savings (in Defined Contribution Plans and Individual Retirement Accounts) and Among Households with Savings, the Median Levels of Savings 2010.

Single-headed households, in contrast, continue to lag behind their married counterparts both in terms of having DC plans or IRAs and in the level of retirement savings. For the population of all households age 50- 64, 60 percent have some DC, IRA, or Keogh savings, according to our analysis of SCF data. However, this varies widely by marital status. Specifically, in 2010, an estimated 71 percent of married households age 50-64 years old had DC,

IRA, and Keogh savings, while only 39 percent and 48 percent of male and female single-headed households had retirement savings, respectively (see fig. 17).[43] Moreover, the median levels of savings among single-headed households were much lower than for married households in this age category in 2010. For married households with retirement savings, the median savings level was $122,560. In contrast, among single men with retirement savings, the median savings level was $50,000. Among single women with retirement savings, the median level of savings was $32,800.

Over One-Third of Married Households Receiving Income from Pensions Opted Not to Receive a Survivor Benefit

Over the last decade, over one-third of married households receiving income from pensions opted not to receive a spousal survivor benefit.[44] There are many reasons why households might decide to opt out of receiving a survivor benefit. For example, a spouse might not be expected to outlive the individual receiving the pension (the participant). Alternatively, the spouse that is expected to survive the spouse receiving the pension might have access to his or her own retirement income. According to our analyses of SCF data, the decision to opt out differed depending on whether the pension participant was the wife or the husband. Specifically, in 2010, 62 percent of men opted for a survivor benefit for their spouse while 38 percent of women did. Men's higher likelihood of choosing survivor benefits could reflect their expectations that their wives are more likely to outlive them, or it could reflect that married women are more likely than married men to need the security of a survivor benefit because of less access to other sources of retirement income.

Several other factors were related to couples' likelihood of opting out of a survivor benefit. Couples with longer marriages were less likely to opt out, possibly reflecting a greater sense of financial responsibility for the surviving spouse among long-lasting marriages. Households in the lowest net worth quintile are more likely to opt out of the survivor benefit than wealthier households. This finding may reflect the fact that households with limited wealth may be unable to afford the benefit reduction that comes with a survivor benefit.[45] Lastly, households with higher levels of assets in DC plans or IRAs were less likely to opt out, perhaps an indicator of the household's level of financial literacy and preparedness overall or simply that, with other retirement savings, the household did not need the higher benefit payment that would result from the couple opting out.[46]

The Decline in Receipt of Spousal Benefits Is Likely to Increase Some Retirees' Economic Vulnerability

Shifts in Marriage and Labor Force Participation Mean Fewer Future Retirees Are Expected to Receive Social Security Spousal Benefits

Looking forward, fewer women will likely receive Social Security spousal benefits because of their declining eligibility based on marital history or increased earnings relative to their husbands, according to SSA projections.[47] More specifically, eligibility for spousal benefits is projected to decline for two reasons. First, the population of women who never marry is projected to more than double in the future. Of women born from 1936 to 1945, 4 percent are projected to never have married by age 70. In contrast, of women born from 1966 to 1975, 10 percent are projected to have never married by age 70.[48] Second, due to the trend toward shorter marriages, fewer elderly divorcees will likely have had a marriage that lasted at least 10 years—an eligibility requirement for divorced spousal benefits. For women who had their first marriage in the early 1960's, 83 percent of marriages lasted at least 10 years, whereas 75 percent of comparable marriages that occurred in the early 1990's lasted this long, according to Census Bureau estimates.[49]

Additionally, due to women's increased lifetime earnings relative to men, fewer women who are eligible for spousal benefits based on their marital history will receive them because they will be eligible for retired worker benefits based on their own work record.[50] Compared to current retirees, more of today's working-age women are likely to receive Social Security benefits based exclusively on their own work history, known as retired worker benefits. Whereas in 1960, 39 percent of women age 62 and older received retired worker benefits, SSA projects that this will increase from 46 percent in 2012 to 62 percent in 2040 (see fig. 18). This increase will largely be driven by the employment and earnings patterns of married and widowed women.

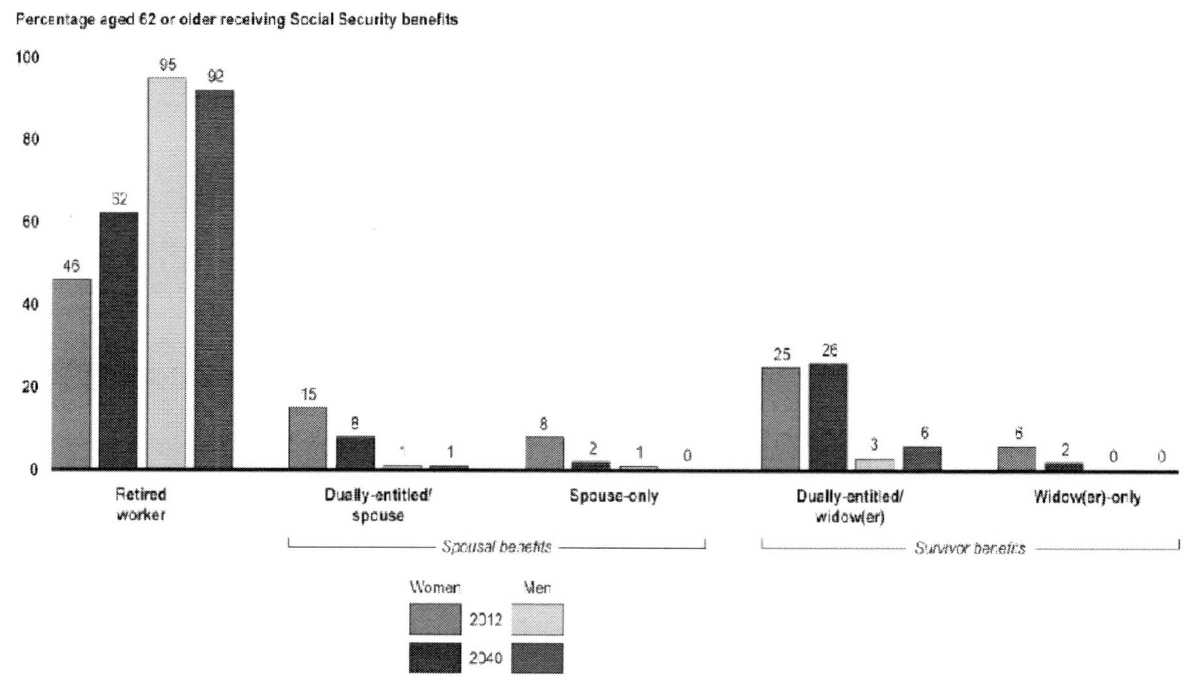

Source: Social Security MINT6 projections.

Note: Due to limitations of the data, the 2012 projections exclude beneficiaries older than 86. As a result, the 2012 data for widows differs from the 2010 data shown in figure 13.

Figure 18. Projected Distribution of Social Security Beneficiary Type by Sex, Age 62 and Older: 2012 to 2040.

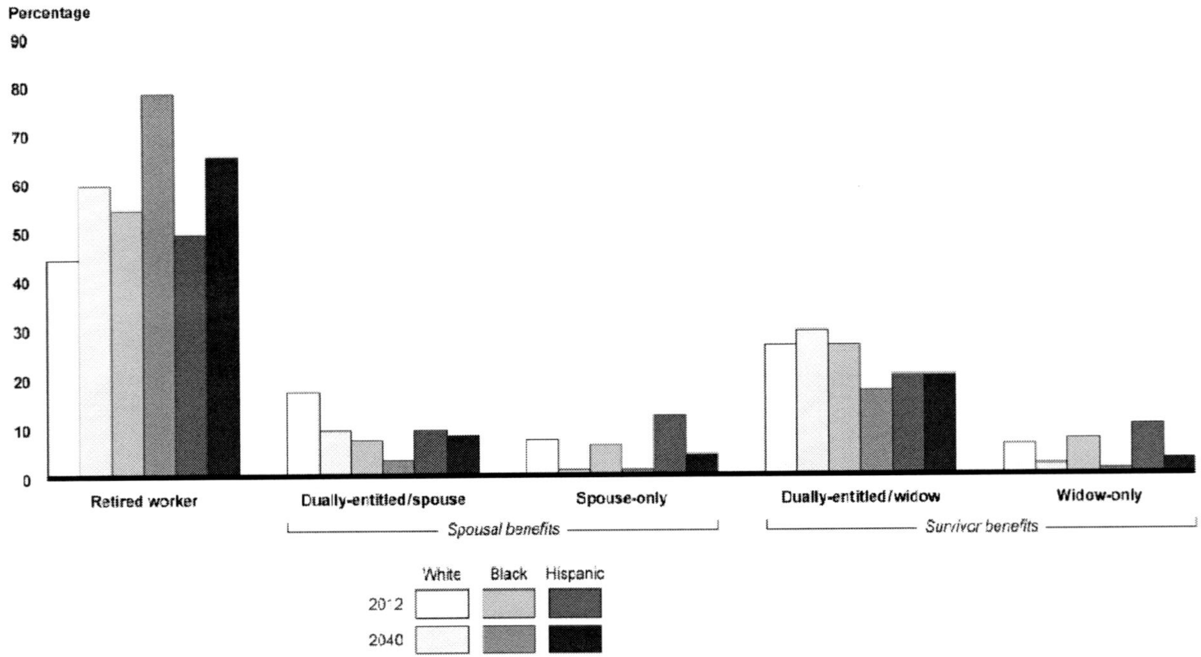

Source: Social Security MINT6 projections.
Note: Due to limitations of the data, the 2012 projections exclude beneficiaries older than 86.

Figure 19. Projected Distribution of Social Security Beneficiary Type for Women by Race, Age 62 and Older: 2012 to 2040.

Over the same period, the proportion of women who are expected to receive benefits based exclusively on marriage— known as spouse-only benefits—is projected to decline from 8 to 2 percent.[51] At the same time, the proportion of women who are expected to receive benefits based on both work history and marriage—known as dually-entitled/spouse benefits—is projected to decrease from 15 to 8 percent. In contrast with today, proportionately more married men are projected to receive survivor benefits in the future due to their decreased earnings relative to their wives. SSA projects that the proportion of men who will receive retired worker benefits will drop by 3 percentage points— from 95 to 92 percent—between 2012 and 2040. At the same time, the proportion of men who are expected to receive survivor benefits based on their marriage to higher-earning wives is projected to increase from 3 to 6 percent (see fig. 18).

Despite these changes, survivor benefits are expected to continue to play an important role for many women. Although the proportion of widows whose benefits will be based solely on marriage—known as widow-only— is projected to decrease from 6 to 2 percent by 2040, SSA projects that the proportion of women who will be dually-entitled widows will remain stable at about one-quarter of all female beneficiaries through 2040 (see fig. 18). This is in part due to the fact that many women who qualify for retired-worker benefits while their husbands are alive (because their retired-worker benefit exceeds 50 percent of their spouse's benefit) will become dually-entitled as widows because their own retired-worker benefit does not exceed 100 percent of their husband's benefit. For example, another analysis projects that two-thirds of wives born from 1966 to 1975 will receive widow benefits rather than their own retired worker benefit when widowed, reflecting women's lower average lifetime earnings relative to their husbands.[52]

In general, the trend away from women receiving spousal benefits is projected to occur across racial and ethnic groups, with the largest shift occurring among black women. According to SSA analyses among whites, blacks, and Hispanics, as of 2012, proportionally, black women were already the most likely to receive retired worker benefits (see fig. 19). Furthermore, between 2012 and 2040, black women are projected to experience the highest growth in this category. In addition, the proportions of dually-entitled/spouse white and black women are projected to decrease by about half between 2012 and 2040, with a small decrease among Hispanic women. Moreover, the proportion of women who are expected to receive widow-only benefits is projected to decrease for all three groups and, by 2040, differ by no more than two percentage points. Unlike these trends, the projections for dually-entitled widows diverge by race. More specifically, the proportion of white dually-entitled widows is projected to increase by 12 percent, while blacks will likely see a 35 percent decrease. These projections do not suggest any change among Hispanic dually-entitled widows.[53]

Current Trends Suggest a Growing Proportion of the Elderly Will Be at Risk of Living in Poverty During Retirement

As the population that is ineligible for spousal and survivor benefits based on marital history—i.e., those who are not married or divorced without a marriage of at least 10 years—is projected to increase, the proportion of people who will depend entirely on their own earnings and savings in retirement is expected to increase as well. For many elderly, women in particular, this shift is likely to be positive, reflecting their higher earnings and greater capacity to save for retirement.

However, elderly with low levels of lifetime earnings, who have no spouse, or who do not receive a spousal benefit—a group that is disproportionately represented by black women—are expected to have correspondingly lower retirement benefits.[54] As a result, a growing proportion of the elderly—especially black women—may be at risk of living in poverty in retirement due to the higher cost of living and lower income associated with being single. As our past work has shown, elderly married individuals have higher levels of median household income and lower poverty rates than those who are never married, divorced, or widowed.[55]

Furthermore, in 2040, the median income levels of this expanding group of never married elderly will continue to be lower than that of their married counterparts, according to SSA projections.

Additionally, even some of those elderly who are eligible to receive spousal benefits may be more economically vulnerable after the death of one spouse due to the trend toward spouses having more similar earnings than in the past. More specifically, the more similar two spouses' earnings, the less likely the survivor is to receive a widow(er) benefit. As seen in figure 20, three hypothetical couples with the same level of preretirement income, but with different earnings ratios, will have very different levels of survivor benefits.[56] The survivor in the one-earner couple receives $1,859 per month—or two-thirds of the previous household benefit at retirement, as determined by the Social Security benefit formula.[57] The survivor in the dual-earner couple with unequal earnings receives 60 percent of the previous household benefit. In contrast, the survivor of the dual-earner couple with equal earnings receives just 50 percent of the previous household benefit—significantly less than at least one measure of what a single person needs to live on relative to what a couple needs.[58]

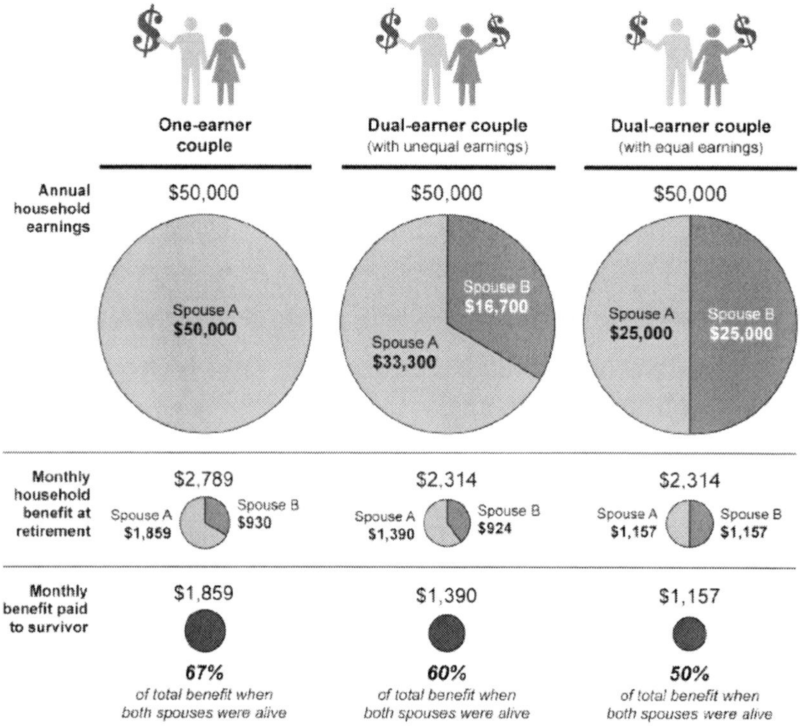

Source: Social Security Administration data and GAO calculations.

Notes: Estimates assume that (1) the monthly equivalent of these annual earnings equals the individual's average indexed monthly earnings used to calculate Social Security benefits; (2) all individuals retire at age 66 in 2013; and (3) there are no cost of living adjustments reflected after the initial benefit is taken at retirement.

Figure 20. Examples of Social Security Retirement and Survivor Income by Household Structure.

Moreover, the proportion of dual-earner wives who are projected to not receive a survivor benefit—because of their relatively high earnings compared to their deceased husbands'—is expected to increase from 18 percent of wives who were born from 1936 to 1945 to 34 percent for wives born from 1966 to 1975.[59] The lower level of survivor benefits generally may affect women for a longer period of time than men, due to women's longer life expectancy. However, working women's increased earnings and personal savings may potentially offset the lower level of survivor benefit, mitigating this issue to some extent.

In addition to the differences in benefit levels among widow(er)s mentioned above, figure 20 also illustrates how retirement benefits can vary while both spouses are alive, for couples with different relative earnings.[60] Namely, a one-earner couple receives a higher total retirement benefit than a dual-earner couple with the same level of household preretirement income. In figure 20, the total monthly benefit for the one-earner couple is $2,789. By contrast, the dual-earner couples receive $2,314, or 17 percent less. As the proportion of one-earner couples continues to decline, however, this disparity will become less and less common.

Some Social Security Policy Options May Offset Effects of Changes in Marital Patterns

Past GAO work has identified a number of options suggested by experts to improve the retirement security of populations vulnerable to poverty by changing the Social Security eligibility rules or benefit structure, although each option has limitations.[61] Some of these options focus specifically on modifying benefits for spouses and survivors, while others would affect broader populations of vulnerable individuals, and may also benefit those affected by changing marital patterns. For example, one option would change the eligibility requirements for divorced spousal benefits by reducing the required length of marriage from 10 to 7 years, with the goal of helping more of the divorced elderly remain out of poverty. Another option would increase benefit amounts for widow(er)s from the current maximum of 67 to 75 percent of the combined amount the couple had received, with the aim of preventing poverty among widow(er)s.[62] This option could be targeted specifically toward low-income survivors by capping the surviving spouse's benefit amount at the average retired worker benefit. However, concerns have been raised that these options may not effectively target other economically vulnerable groups like low-income Social Security retired worker recipients who never married. Further, both of these options could provide benefits to higher-income elderly who may not be particularly economically vulnerable.

Other reform options target the vulnerable population of low-income people who do not qualify for spousal or survivor benefits, such as those who never marry, and who would otherwise receive retired worker benefits. Retired worker benefits are generally calculated on the basis of a worker's average indexed monthly earnings for the worker's highest 35 years of earnings. While Social Security's benefit structure is progressive, meaning that its retirement benefits replace a higher percentage of earnings for lower-income workers, a lifetime low-wage worker would still have correspondingly low benefits. Furthermore, the current benefit formula does not distinguish between low average wages caused by low lifetime earnings or low average wages caused by years of unemployment. One set of proposed options aims to increase benefit adequacy for lifetime low wage workers by increasing the level of the Special Minimum Primary Insurance Amount (also referred to as the "Special Minimum Benefit")—a minimum Social Security benefit that is based on the number of years a worker has spent in Social Security-covered employment. The Special Minimum Benefit is paid to an eligible retired worker if it is higher than the benefit amount computed using the typical Social Security benefit formula based on the worker's highest 35 years of earnings.[63] Increasing the Special Minimum Benefit could help more elderly avoid poverty.[64] However, it is difficult to effectively target lifetime low earners with this option because it is possible for high-wage earners who work part-time or sporadically to accumulate 11 years of covered employment—the minimum required under current law to qualify for the Special Minimum Benefit.

In addition to revising the Special Minimum Benefit, another option targets those who have shorter periods of covered employment because they were providing care to a family member and do not qualify for spousal benefits. More specifically, this option could change the Social Security benefit structure to provide earnings credits to caregivers (known as caregiver credits) during years in which they do not have earnings because they were providing care to children or elderly relatives. However, according to experts, this option may not reach its target population either because, for example, low-income people are less likely to take time out of the labor market to provide care for a family member. Consequently, people who have relatively higher incomes may benefit more from the creation of caregiver credits.

These policy options have costs that would place greater strains on the Social Security trust funds, which are already projected to have significantly depleted assets by 2033, at which time claimants would only receive 77 percent of their entitled benefits. The cost each option might impose varies depending on several factors, including: (1) the number of additional beneficiaries that would become eligible, (2) whether other additional adjustments—such as including a minimum work requirement for divorced spouses—would be included, and (3) their potential to offset the new costs.

The administrative burdens associated with implementing such changes are also important factors. For example, caregiver credits would be complex to administer due to the challenges associated with verifying that care was provided to a qualifying person and the amount of care that was provided.

The Shift Away from Defined Benefit Plans Also Increases the Economic Vulnerability of Elderly Spouses

The transition in private employer plan sponsorship from DB to DC plans has increased the vulnerability of spouses due to differences in the level of spousal protections between these retirement plans. While over half of U.S. workers do not participate in employer-sponsored pension plans,[65] those with spouses who do participate may have different federal protections depending on whether their spouse participates in a DB or DC plan. In DB plans, current law requires spousal consent if the participant wishes to waive the survivor annuity for his or her spouse. In contrast, under DC plans, there is generally no federal requirement to provide an annuity option and participants do not need spousal consent to withdraw funds from the account—either before or at retirement. While spouses are generally required to be the default beneficiary of the remaining account balance upon the death of the participant, there is no protection against the assets being invested unwisely, inadvertently spent down too quickly, or simply withdrawn fully upon a job change and rolled into an IRA, with a change in beneficiary. In a worst case scenario, the spouse who participates in the DC plan could withdraw all the assets and spend them in ways that do not provide for the couple's retirement security. While the increases in dual-earner couples and women's coverage under DC plans have the potential to mitigate these concerns by providing alternative sources of retirement income, spouses with lower or no earnings may remain vulnerable.

To address this vulnerability, some policy analysts have suggested strengthening spousal protections in DC plans. 66 For example, requiring spousal consent for a participant to roll over a DC plan account to an IRA—which is not required to make the spouse the beneficiary of the account balance upon the owner's death—or to cash out the account altogether, would allow spouses a level of input similar to the legal provisions governing DB plans. However, according to some experts, the administrative burden of obtaining spousal consent for such modifications to DC plans would impose administrative costs on plan sponsors and could slow down the retirement process. For example, one expert explained that DC plan benefit elections can be done electronically and in a matter of days. In contrast, DB plan elections typically take about 30 days, in part because the pen and paper process of obtaining notarized spousal consent in order to elect something other than a qualified joint and survivor annuity (QJSA) holds up the process.[67] Additionally, one agency official we interviewed questioned the need for DC plans to adopt spousal consent features, pointing out that spousal protections under DB plans were instituted to protect nonworking spouses at a time when women generally did not have the same level of access to and participation in retirement plans as they do today.[68]

Despite their relatively greater level of spousal protections, some policy advocates have also proposed revising spousal provisions that apply to DB plans. First, similar to the concern that the Social Security survivor benefit amount is too low, one expert has suggested increasing the minimum amount for DB survivor annuities from 50 percent to at least two-thirds of the prior annuity amount. Such a change would help surviving spouses better maintain their standard of living. However, such a change would entail lowering the initial annuity amount, which may be a hardship for some retirees and could deter some participants from electing the QJSA. Another policy option would seek to remedy the unequal treatment of widow(er)s under DB QJSAs. Typically, in a QJSA, the amount of the annuity that the couple receives while both spouses are alive does not change if the worker's spouse dies first. In other words, the worker would see no change in DB household income if widowed. On the other hand, if the worker dies first, the annuity amount that the surviving spouse receives may be reduced to as little as 50 percent of the prior amount. To remedy this imbalance, two experts have suggested paying the widow(er) a predetermined amount, regardless of which spouse dies first. This "symmetric" joint and survivor annuity option is currently available for plan sponsors to offer, but they generally have not done so. Accordingly, one version of this policy option would be to make this option the normal form of benefit for married participants, requiring spousal consent to opt for a different form of payment. A symmetric joint and survivor annuity has the advantage of requiring a smaller benefit reduction on account of the survivor benefit than a standard joint and survivor annuity, which could lead to more participants taking this option. However, one agency official noted that employers expressed concern that beneficiaries with this option might not report the death of their spouse to avoid incurring any benefit reduction.

CONCLUSION

Over the last 50 years, major societal changes in the United States have had important consequences for how Americans live, work, and save for retirement. Indeed, unlike in decades past, fewer people are getting married, and those who do often marry later in life and for shorter periods. These trends have consequences for economic security because unmarried individuals are unable to take advantage of the economic benefits and efficiencies of marriage and may therefore be at greater risk of poverty in old age. Moreover, these trends have disproportionately occurred within the nation's most vulnerable populations—low-income, less-educated, and some minorities. If these trends continue, many Americans' economic security—both in their working years and in old age—could further deteriorate.

While marriage rates overall have declined, the role women play in the labor market has expanded. As a result, women have become major contributors to household income and household retirement savings. For many households, these gains could enhance economic security in old age. However, low-wage workers who never marry or were not married long enough to qualify for Social Security spousal benefits may not be able to accrue sufficient retirement savings to offset the lack of a spousal benefit in old age. Even within two-earner households, the Social Security survivor benefit declines as earnings for both spouses become more similar. Survivors are therefore likely to depend on other forms of retirement income to maintain their standard of living prior to their spouse's death. Further, the shift to DC plans—which typically offer fewer protections for spouses and fewer possibilities for participants to annuitize within their plans—will likely result in more retirees outliving their assets.

These trends and their consequences raise important questions for existing programs, such as Social Security, and current protections for spouses in pension plans. As part of any future reform efforts in these areas, it will be important for policy makers to consider these trends in order to minimize poverty and ensure retirement security among the elderly.

AGENCY COMMENTS

We provided a draft of this report to the Department of Labor, the Department of the Treasury, and the Social Security Administration for review and comment. While none of the agencies provided official comments, the Department of Labor and the Department of the Treasury provided technical comments, which we incorporated as appropriate.

Sincerely yours,
Charles A. Jeszeck Director
Education, Workforce, and Income Security

APPENDIX I: OBJECTIVES, SCOPE, AND METHODS

To analyze trends in marriage and labor force participation and their implications for retirement security, we examined: (1) the trends in and status of marriage and labor force participation in the American household; (2) how those trends have affected spousal benefits and retirement savings behavior within households; and (3) what the implications of these trends are for retirement security. This appendix provides a detailed account of the information and methods we used to answer these questions. Section 1 describes the key information sources pertaining to analyses we conducted for each reporting objective. Sections 2 and 3 provide additional information on the characteristics of the individuals and households we analyzed for Objective 2.

Section 1: Information Sources

To address our objectives, we obtained information from a variety of sources. We obtained and analyzed data from: (1) U.S. Census Bureau (Census) and Bureau of Labor Statistics (BLS) reports; (2) the Integrated Public Use Microdata Series (IPUMS) data consisting of decennial Census data and American Community Survey data; (3) the Survey of Income and Program Participation (SIPP) public use and restricted Gold Standard data,[1] (4) the Current Population Survey; (5) the Survey of Consumer Finances (SCF); (6) SSA's Modeling Income in the Near Term model; and (7) SSA's actuarial estimates. Table 3 summarizes the data sources used to address each objective. To inform our data analyses for all three objectives, we obtained additional information from (1) prior GAO reports and the academic literature on trends in marriage, labor force participation, and retirement income; (2) relevant federal laws and regulations, and (3) a range of experts in the area of retirement security. This section provides a description of the information sources, how we used them, and the steps we took to ensure their reliability.

Table 3. Data Sources Used for Each Reporting Objective

Objective	Data sources
Objective 1: Trends in marriage and labor force participation	• Census Bureau and Bureau of Labor Statistics reports • Integrated Public Use Microdata Series (consisting of decennial Census data andAmerican Community Survey data) • Survey of Income and Program Participation public-use data
Objective 2: Receipt of spousal benefits and household retirement savings behavior	• Survey of Income and Program Participation public-use and restricted-use Gold Standard data • Survey of Consumer Finances
Objective 3: Implications of these trends for future retirement security	• Modeling Income in the Near Term model • SSA actuarial estimates

Source: GAO.

Census and BLS Reports

To understand trends in marital status, single parenthood, and labor force participation over time, which are reported in Objective 1 of the report, we compiled and analyzed data from a number of published Census and BLS reports. The data in these reports draw upon Census and BLS surveys including: the U.S. Census Bureau, Current Population Reports; the Survey of Income and Program Participation; and the Annual Social and Economic Supplements, Current Population Survey.

Integrated Public Use Microdata Series (IPUMS)

To understand the relationship between income and education and trends in marriage and single-parenthood from 1960 to 2010, in Objective 1 we analyzed the Integrated Public Use Microdata Series (IPUMS). IPUMS consists of more than fifty high-precision samples of the American population drawn from fifteen federal censuses and from the American Community Surveys of 2000-2011. Together these samples constitute a rich source of quantitative information on long-term changes in the American population. IPUMS assigns uniform codes across all the samples and provides documentation for each data set.

In our analysis of IPUMS data (Figures 7 and 8), the data points for years 1960, 1970, 1980, 1990 and 2000 are from the decennial Census, and data points for the year 2010 are from the American Community Survey.

Weights and Standard Error Calculations in IPUMS Data

For all our analyses of IPUMS data, we used person weights. To estimate standard errors, we followed procedures recommended by IPUMS methodological guidance papers. We applied the appropriate design factors provided in Census Bureau publications for each year of data, taking into account the population subsamples on which we conducted our analysis.

Survey of Income and Program Participation

To answer parts of Objectives 1 and 2, we analyzed data collected through the SIPP, a nationally representative survey conducted by Census that collects detailed information on marital history and caregiving, among many other areas. Specifically, we used the data to analyze trends in (1) the characteristics of women that do not have a marriage that would qualify them for Social Security spousal benefits and (2) women's time spent out of the workforce providing childcare. The SIPP survey is conducted in a series of national panels, each of which is collected for multiple years. Within each panel, the data are collected in a series of "waves" which take place in 4 month cycles. Within each wave, Census administers a core survey consisting of questions that are asked at every interview, and several modules relating to a particular topic. We used data from the core survey, the topical module on marital history, and the topical module on employment history from two SIPP panels, the 1996 and 2008 panels. The 1996 panel, which was collected between April 1996 and March 2000, contained approximately 40,000 interviews at the beginning of the survey. The 2008 panel, which was collected between September 2008 and December 2012, contained approximately 52,000 interviews at the beginning of the survey. For both panels, the topical module on employment history was administered in Wave 1, and the topical module on marital history was administered in Wave 2. In each wave, we analyzed data from the fourth interview month. For the 1996 panel, the Wave 1 data was collected between March and June of 1996, and the Wave 2 data was collected between July and October of 1996. For the 2008 panel, the Wave 1 data was collected between August and November of 2008, and the Wave 2 data was collected between December 2008 and March 2009.

Weights and Standard Error Calculations in SIPP

For all of the SIPP analyses, we used SIPP individual-level weights to compute point estimates. Because our analysis of the SIPP public use data involves merging data for individuals from multiple waves, we chose not to use SIPP replicate weights, as the replicate weight analysis becomes complex and computationally burdensome under these circumstances. Instead we used Stata's survey data analysis package to declare a survey design for the data, using the following survey design variables from the SIPP data: GHLFSAM (half-sample code) to indicate the primary sampling unit, and GVARSTR (variance stratum code) to indicate the strata. GAO internal analysis has shown that using these survey design variables yields estimated standard errors that are very similar to those produced using the SIPP replicate weights.

SIPP Analysis of Women with Qualifying Marriages

To analyze the characteristics of women who had not attained a marriage that would qualify them for Social Security spousal benefits, we used information from the marital history modules of the 1996 and 2008 SIPP panels. We classified a woman as attaining a qualifying marriage if she either a) was currently married at the time of the survey, or b) was not currently married, but had previously been in a marriage that lasted for at least 10 years. We used data from the marital history module on the start and end date of marriages to determine whether a marriage had lasted at least 10 years. Because the public use data does not contain the month of marriage, we could not know precisely how long each person had been married. For women whose marriages were close to the 10-year mark, we had to choose between making our classification err on the side of overly inclusive or overly exclusive. We chose to define a marriage as lasting at least 10 years if the difference between the year of marriage termination and the year of initiation was at least 11. This means that we did not include any women whose marriage was less than 10 years. However, we did exclude some women whose marriage was exactly 10 years. For example, a woman who married in January 2000 and divorced in February 2010 would have a 10 year marriage, but our classification excluded her. We made this choice to avoid incorrectly including women with marriages less than 10 years. For example, if we defined our classification using the rule that the difference between the termination date and the start date was 10 years, we would include women who married in December 2000 and divorced in January 2010—a marriage that lasted 9 years and 2 months.

We analyzed the characteristics of men and women who had attained a marriage that would qualify them for Social Security spousal benefits by comparing qualifying marriage rates across different demographic groups (specifically, across different age, racial and ethnic groups, education level, and income categories.) In addition, to examine whether the relationship between race and qualifying marriage rates remained when controlling for income and education, we also ran several multivariate regressions on women age 55-64. We ran probit regressions of the probability of attaining a qualifying marriage for women on race with controls for income and education. We also ran probit regressions of the probability of attaining a qualifying marriage on race interacted with income, and on race interacted with education. These regressions show the negative relationship between a person being in the "black" race category and attaining a qualifying marriage remains statistically significant, even with controls for income and education, in both 1996 and 2008. Similarly, we ran probit regressions of the probability of being currently married on race with controls for education and income, and we also ran probit regressions of the probability of being currently married on race interacted with income, and on race interacted with education, for women age 55-64 in 1996 and 2008. These regressions show that the negative relationship between a person being in the "black" race category and being currently married remained significant with controls for education and income.

SIPP Analysis of Time Spent out of the Workforce to Provide Childcare

To analyze women's time spent out of the workforce providing childcare, we used data from the 2008 SIPP employment history module, combined with data from the fertility history module. We used the fertility history module to obtain information about whether an individual had ever had a child. This was necessary because we were looking at a person's lifetime employment, and many older people who have taken time out of the workforce for childcare in the past do not currently have children living with them. We restricted this analysis to women age 20-62 who had worked for at least 6 months prior to the birth of their first child. We set this age range because the SIPP "time off for caregiving" questions were only asked for people in this age range. We also restricted the analysis to women whose first child was born in 2004 or earlier. This restriction was made so that all women in the analysis would have given birth at least 4 years before the survey interview. We then examined the length of time women took out of the workforce, during their first spell out of the workforce. We restricted our analysis to the first spell out of the workforce in order to mitigate the impact of older women being more likely to have had multiple children, and therefore multiple spells out of the workforce, compared to younger women. We created five categories for time spent out of the workforce. The top category was "4 or more years". We made this the top category so that all women in the analysis were interviewed at least 4 years since the birth of their first child, and therefore would have had the opportunity to have taken off 4 or more years.

SIPP Analysis Comparing Characteristics of Female Beneficiaries

For our analysis in Objective 2 comparing the characteristics of women who receive Social Security spouse-only benefits with those receiving retired-worker benefits or dually-entitled spouse benefits, we used the 2008 SIPP restricted-use Gold Standard data. We used the Gold Standard SIPP data because, despite its advantages, the SIPP public-use data has one main limitation for our analysis. As with most survey data, SIPP public-use data are self-reported. This can be problematic for the reporting of data on income sources and the type of Social Security benefits individuals receive. For example, respondents might incorrectly report that they receive a spousal benefit, when in fact they are receiving a retired-worker benefit. To mitigate this problem, we used the 2008 SIPP Gold Standard data. Census created this file by extracting variables from the SIPP panels conducted in 2008 and merging SSA-provided administrative data including the Summary Earnings Records, Detailed Earnings Records, and the Master Beneficiary Record. Census refers to these data as the Gold Standard because they represent the available confidential micro-data that would be used for analysis by an authorized researcher working in a restricted-access facility.

Survey of Consumer Finances

To answer part of Objective 2, we analyzed data from the 2010 SCF. Specifically, we used the data to analyze (1) the decision to opt out of a survivor benefit among married households with pension income, and (2) retirement savings behavior among married and single-headed households. The SCF is a triennial, nationally representative survey from the Board of Governors of the Federal Reserve System (Federal Reserve). The 2010 SCF surveyed 6,482 households about their pensions, incomes, labor force participation, asset holdings and debts, use of financial services, and demographic information. For the purposes of this report, a household refers to the primary economic unit within a household, which the SCF refers to as a family. To estimate the age, marital status, net worth, income, and participation in a DC or DB plan, we relied on variable definitions used for Federal Reserve publications using the SCF and consulted with an agency official.[2]

To analyze the decision to opt out of a survivor benefit, we conducted both comparisons of means and cross-tabulations, and ran some simple regression analyses using the SCF. Our regression analyses were logit models which predicted the probability of a person choosing a survivor benefit as a function of net worth and total retirement liquid assets (in separate regressions). In our regression of survivor benefit choice on net worth, we grouped net worth into quartiles, and constructed categorical variables for each quartile. We included retirement liquid assets as a continuous variable.

The SCF is subject to non-sampling error and non-response, which can influence the accuracy of point and variance estimates. To address this, the Federal Reserve provides a set of implicate data—which contain information about imputed variables—and a replicate weight file, which permits users of the SCF microdata to obtain more accurate variance estimates. We followed Federal Reserve guidance and used both the implicate data and the replicate weights when constructing our point estimates and standard error estimates, both in our univariate analyses and in our regression analyses.

Modeling Income in the Near Term

To project the distribution of Social Security beneficiary types for women into the future for Objective 3, officials from the Office of Retirement Policy at the Social Security Administration (SSA) provided GAO with projections based on simulations they conducted with the Modeling Income in the Near Term model, Version 6 (MINT6). This model is used to make projections related to individuals' retirement income, marital trends, Social Security benefits, and poverty. The MINT6 is built from Census survey data and Social Security's own administrative records.[3]

Social Security Actuarial Estimates

The Office of the Chief Actuary at the Social Security Administration provided GAO with the data used in Objective 3, figure 20, which presents examples of Social Security Retirement and Survivor Income benefit levels for households with different hypothetical earnings configurations (i.e. one-earner couples, dual-earner couples with unequal earnings, and dual-earner couples with equal earnings).

Sampling Error

Estimates from the surveys described above are subject to sampling error because these surveys are probability samples based on random selections. Since each possible sample could have provided different estimates, we express our confidence in the precision of the sample results as 95 percent confidence intervals. These intervals would contain the actual population values for 95 percent of the samples that could have been drawn. In this report, we report all percentage or other numerical estimates along with their 95 percent confidence intervals. In addition, any differences between point estimates presented in this report are statistically significant at the 95 percent confidence level unless otherwise noted.

Data Reliability and Limitations

For the IPUMS, SIPP public-use and Gold Standard data, SCF and MINT6 data described above, we conducted a data reliability assessment of selected variables by conducting electronic data tests for completeness and accuracy, reviewing documentation on the dataset, or interviewing knowledgeable officials about how the data are collected and maintained and their appropriate uses. When we learned that particular fields were not reliable or were not consistently reported, we did not use them. For the purposes of our analysis, we found the variables that we ultimately reported on to be sufficiently reliable.

Nonetheless, our analysis of nationally representative survey data had several limitations. The SCF and other surveys that are based on self-reported data are subject to several other sources of non-sampling error, including the inability to get information about all sample cases; difficulties of definition;

differences in the interpretation of questions; respondents' inability or unwillingness to provide correct information; and errors made in collecting, recording, coding, and processing data. These non-sampling errors can influence the accuracy of information presented in the report, although the magnitude of their effect is not known.

We also encountered limitations specific to our study. First, in using the 2008 SIPP Gold Standard Data to analyze the characteristics of female Social Security beneficiaries, we were unable to analyze information for approximately 6 percent of the female respondents age 62 and over who did not provide their Social Security numbers because Census uses the SSN to match the information respondents provide in the SIPP survey with the information from administrative files.[4] Second, in using the SCF to evaluate changes in the retirement savings behavior of households, we were unable to analyze the decisions of households to opt out of the survivor benefit prior to 2001 due to changes in the SCF questionnaire. In addition, in using the SCF to analyze near-retirement households, we widened the age range we examined from 55-64 to 50-64 in some instances to improve the precision of our estimates.

Literature Review and Interviews

To gain an understanding of the trends in marriage and labor force participation and their implications for retirement security, we conducted an extensive literature review and interviewed a range of experts. To identify existing studies, we used online research software to search through databases of scholarly and peer-reviewed materials for information on these topics, including articles, journals, reports, and studies dating back to 2002. In addition, we reviewed articles that were collected during the previous GAO study on women's retirement security that contained relevant information and reviewed articles that were suggested to us by the experts we interviewed.[5] The articles we cited in the report were reviewed for methodological adequacy by at least two GAO analysts with expertise in social science methods.

To supplement the literature review, we conducted interviews with experts. To ensure that we obtained a balanced perspective, we interviewed 49 experts with a range of perspectives and from 21 different types of organizations including government, academia, advocacy groups, think tanks and industry. We also consulted several of these experts on technical issues related to our analysis. We identified and interviewed experts who have specialized knowledge about spousal protections and retirement security in a specific area of expertise (e.g., law or social science), or who were recommended by one or more people or groups we had previously interviewed. Specifically, we interviewed federal agency officials at the Departments of the Treasury and Labor, the Social Security Administration, the Census Bureau, and the Office of Management and Budget; academic experts and subject-matter experts at Drexel University, the Employee Benefit Research Institute, Syracuse University, and the Urban Institute; and industry experts and advocates from AARP, the American Benefits Council, Global Policy Solutions, the Institute for Women's Policy Research, the Investment Company Institute, Mercer, the National Women's Law Center, the National Gay and Lesbian Task Force, the National Hispanic Council on Aging, the Pension Rights Center, and the Women's Institute for a Secure Retirement.

To identify the policy options that may address retirement security issues under Social Security and private employer-sponsored plans, we reviewed past GAO reports and interviewed experts. For the Social Security options, we reviewed GAO's prior work in this area.[6] We selected options that focus on either spousal or survivor benefits or, more broadly, on elderly populations that are vulnerable to poverty. We identified policy options that would seek to address spousal protections in private employer-sponsored DB and DC plans through interviews with retirement policy experts representing a range of perspectives and from different types of organizations including government, academia, advocacy groups, and the private sector. The Social Security, DB, and DC policy options listed in this report are not intended to be exhaustive and we are not recommending or endorsing the adoption of any particular policy option. Rather, we identified them as potential options for policymakers to consider, along with other relevant proposals, as they address retirement security issues. In addition, for this report, we did not conduct an independent analysis of the potential legal effects of these policy options.

SECTION 2: ANALYSIS OF THE CHARACTERISTICS OF SOCIAL SECURITY SPOUSAL BENEFICIARIES

To compare the characteristics of female Social Security beneficiaries in Objective 2, we used a sample of beneficiaries from the SIPP Gold Standard data set. Table 4 provides descriptive information on the population of the beneficiaries we analyzed by categories of beneficiaries, including (1) all female Social Security beneficiaries (including widows); (2) retired-worker, non-widow beneficiaries; (3) spouse-only beneficiaries; and (4) dually-entitled workers. We removed the widows from the sample of retired workers so that we could compare a similar set of female beneficiaries (i.e. all non-widows).

Table 5 provides information on the wealth and income characteristics of all female Social Security beneficiaries that were married at the time of the survey. Again, by restricting the sample to women who are in similar life circumstances (i.e. married), we can obtain a more accurate picture of the wealth and income levels of spouse-only beneficiaries (who are by definition married), relative to their married counterparts in the retired-worker and dually-entitled categories.

SECTION 3: ANALYSIS OF THE CHARACTERISTICS OF MARRIED HOUSEHOLDS THAT OPT OUT OF SURVIVOR BENEFITS

To understand the characteristics of married households that opt not to receive a survivor benefit for Objective 2, we analyzed a sample of married households currently receiving pension income from the SCF data. To identify these households, we used three questions from the SCF survey. Specifically, we selected households that:

- Responded to "Is anyone in the household receiving pension benefits currently?" with "Yes";
- Responded to "Is this pension currently an account plan, such as a 401(k), where you could take the whole balance as one payment if you wanted to?" with "No;" and
- Responded to "Is this a payment or account from a current job, past job, a disability or military benefit, former spouse's pension, or something else?" with either "Current job pension of respondent or spouse/partner," "Past job pension of respondent or spouse/partner (except military)" or "Disability."

Among the households that are currently receiving pension benefits, we identified households that opted for a survivor benefit by using an additional question from the SCF survey.

Table 4. Characteristics of Female Social Security Beneficiaries: 2011

	All female Social Security beneficiaries (including widows)		Retired workers (excluding widows)[a]		Spouse-only		Dually-entitled spouse	
	Mean or Percent	Standard error	Mean or Percent	Standard error	Mean or Percent	Standard error	Mean or Percent	Standard error
Age (years)	71.7	0.06	68.2	0.12	70.6	0.28	69.4	0.22
Marital status (percent)								
Never married	4	0.3	10	1	0	—	0	—
Married	47	0.5	68	1	95	1	91	1
Divorced	13	0.5	22	1	5	1	9	1
Widowed	36	0.5	—	—	0	—	0	—
Number of children	2.7	0.02	2.2	0.03	3.1	0.09	2.8	0.06
Race and ethnicity (percent)								
White, Non-Hispanic	81	0.4	79	1	81	2	90	1
Black, Non-Hispanic	9	0.2	10	0.5	3	1	3	1
Hispanic	6	0.3	7	1	11	2	4	1
Other, Non-Hispanic	4	0.2	4	0.4	5	1	3	1
Education level (percent)								
No high school diploma	13	0.5	8	1	20	2	8	1
High school diploma	37	0.7	31	1	43	2	43	2
Some college	30	0.6	34	1	19	2	30	1
Bachelor's degree or higher	20	0.5	27	1	18	2	19	1
Individual lifetime earnings (2012 $)	$721,333	$7,982	$1,110,413	$15,580	$162,206	$12,747	$395,176	$11,507
Household lifetime earnings (2012 $)	$1,737,804	$42,050	$2,449,516	$102,672	$2,307,574	$118,324	$2,734,215	$82,496
Own home (percent)	84	0.5	85	1	87	2	91	1
Observations[b]		6701		2443		627		853

Source: GAO analysis of SIPP Gold Standard data.

Note: Due to federal confidentiality requirements intended to protect the privacy of survey respondents, Census is not permitted to release maximum and minimum values of variables from the SIPP restricted Gold Standard data.

[a] We removed the widows from the sample of retired workers so that we could compare a similar set of female beneficiaries (i.e. all non widows) since the spouse-only and dually-entitled spouse beneficiary categories by definition do not include widows.

[b] Some variables had a lower number of observations, due to lower response rates for particular segments of the SIPP survey.

Table 5. Comparison of Wealth and Income Characteristics of Married Female Social Security Beneficiaries: 2011

	Married retired workers (excluding widows)		Married spouse-only		Married dually-entitled spouse	
	Percent	**Standard error**	**Percent**	**Standard error**	**Percent**	**Standard error**
Own home	94	1	89	2	93	1
Total net worth categories						
Less than or equal to $150,000	28	1	32	2	23	2
Greater than $150,000 through $300,000	21	1	17	1	20	2
Greater than $300,000 through $450,000	13	1	15	1	15	1
Greater than $450,000 through $600,000	8	1	7	1	8	1
Greater than $600,000	30	1	29	2	34	2
Home equity categories						
Less than or equal to $75,000	27	1	32	2	22	1
Greater than $75,000 through $150,000	24	1	22	2	26	2
Greater than $150,000 through $225,000	15	1	12	2	15	1

Table 5. (Continued)

	Married retired workers (excluding widows)		Married spouse-only		Married dually-entitled spouse	
	Percent	**Standard error**	**Percent**	**Standard error**	**Percent**	**Standard error**
Greater than $225,000 through $300,000	11	1	10	1	12	1
Greater than $300,000	23	1	23	2	25	2
Household lifetime earnings categories						
Less than or equal to $750,000	5	1	11	1	4	1
Greater than $750,000 through $1,500,000	10	1	21	2	7	1
Greater than $1,500,000 through $2,250,000	17	1	26	2	22	2
Greater than $2,250,000	68	1	42	2	68	2
Observations	1594		580		764	

Source: GAO analysis of SIPP Gold Standard data.

Note: Due to federal confidentiality requirements intended to protect the privacy of survey respondents, Census is not permitted to release maximum and minimum values of variables from the SIPP Gold Standard data. Some variables had a lower number of observations, due to lower response rates for particular segments of the SIPP survey. Some within group percentages do not total 100 due to rounding.

Specifically, we selected households that:

- Responded to "If you were to die, what percent of this current retirement payment would your spouse/partner continue to receive?" with "Start at a later time, no indication of reduced benefit," "Start at a later time, indication of reduced benefit," "Lump sum payout," "Full amount for limited period," "Full amount, no time limit or time period not specified," or "other."

To ensure that we categorized these households appropriately, we consulted an official at the Federal Reserve.

Table 6 presents descriptive information on the characteristics of married households currently receiving pension income (presented in the third column) as well as on all households currently receiving pension income (presented in the middle column).

Table 6. Characteristics of Households Currently Receiving Pension Income

	Percentage of all households	Percentage of all marriedhouseholds
Age of household head		
Under 45 years old	2%	2%
45-54 years old	5%	5%
55-64 years old	22%	26%
65-69 years old	17%	22%
70-79 years old	33%	30%
80 years and older	21%	15%
Marital status		
Married	54%	100%
Living with partner	2%	0%
Separated	1%	0%
Divorced	13%	0%
Widowed	26%	0%
Never married	4%	0%
Current length of marriage		
0-10 years	NA	12%
11-20 years	NA	10%
21-40 years	NA	35%
Over 40 years	NA	42%

Table 6. (Continued)

	Percentage of all households	Percentage of all marriedhouseholds
Age of spouse/partner		
18-34 years old	NA	1%
35-44 years old	NA	2%
45-54 years old	NA	12%
55-64 years old	NA	32%
65-69 years old	NA	20%
70-79 years old	NA	25%
80 years and older	NA	7%
Race/ethnicity of household head		
White non-Hispanic	83%	85%
Black	11%	8%
Hispanic	2%	3%
Other	3%	3%
Education of household head		
No high school diploma/GED	10%	9%
High school diploma or GED	36%	32%
Some college	17%	18%
College degree or more	38%	41%
Household income bracket		
< $25,000	21%	7%
$25,000-$49,999	32%	30%
$50,000-$74,999	21%	24%
$75,000-$99,999	10%	13%
$100,000 - $249,999	14%	22%
$250,000 or greater	2%	4%
Household net worth bracket		
< $50,000	18%	10%
$50,000 - $199,999	28%	25%
$200,000 - $399,999	20%	23%
$400,000 - $999,999	21%	26%
$1,000,000 - $1,999,999	9%	11%
$2,000,000 or greater	4%	5%

Source: GAO analysis of 2010 Survey of Consumer Finances data.

Table notes: Due to limitations in the SCF data, households in the above analysis include both households that are currently receiving retirement income from a defined benefit plan or have chosen to annuitize their defined contribution benefits. The estimates presented in this table have 95 percent confidence intervals that are within +/- 2.10 percentage points of the estimate itself. Some within group percentages do not total 100 due to rounding.

To understand the savings behavior of working-age households for Objective 2, we analyzed a sample of working-age households from the SCF data. Table 7 presents descriptive information on all of the working-age households and married households in this sample.

Table 7. Characteristics of Working-age Households

	Percentage of all households	**Percentage of all marriedhouseholds**
Age of household head		
18-34 years old	27%	19%
35-44 years old	23%	26%
45-54 years old	27%	31%
55-64 years old	23%	25%
Marital status		
Married	51%	100%
Living with partner	9%	0%
Separated	3%	0%
Divorced	14%	0%
Widowed	3%	0%
Never married	19%	0%
Age of spouse/partner		
18-34 years old	NA	24%
35-44 years old	NA	27%
45-54 years old	NA	30%
55-64 years old	NA	17%
65-69 years old	NA	1%
70-79 years or older	NA	0%
Race/ethnicity of household head		
White non-Hispanic	68%	74%
Black	15%	8%
Hispanic	13%	13%
Other	5%	5%
Education of household head		
No high school diploma/GED	10%	9%
High school diploma or GED	31%	30%
Some college	20%	18%
College degree or more	39%	43%

Table 7. (Continued)

	Percentage of all households	Percentage of all marriedhouseholds
Household type		
Married	51%	100%
Living with partner	9%	0%
Female single-headed	24%	0%
Male single-headed	16%	0%
Labor force participation[a]		
Male 1-earner household	29%	27%
Female 1-earner household	23%	6%
2-earner household	39%	64%
0-earner household	9%	4%
Household income bracket		
< $25,000	24%	10%
$25,000-$49,999	27%	20%
$50,000-$74,999	18%	21%
$75,000-$99,999	11%	16%
$100,000 - $249,999	16%	26%
$250,000 or greater	4%	7%
Household net worth bracket		
< $50,000	49%	34%
$50,000 - $199,999	23%	26%
$200,000 - $399,999	11%	14%
$400,000 - $999,999	9%	13%
$1,000,000 - $1,999,999	4%	6%
$2,000,000 or greater	4%	7%
Balanceof retirement savings accounts[b]		
<$25,000	68%	55%
$25,000 - $49,999	7%	9%
$50,000 - $99,999	7%	10%
$100,000 - $249,999	8%	13%
$250,000 - $499,999	4%	7%
$500,000 - $999,999	2%	4%
$1,000,000 or more	1%	2%

Source: GAO analysis of 2010 Survey of Consumer Finances data.

Table notes: The estimates presented in this table have 95 percent confidence intervals that are within +/- 1.06 percentage points of the estimate itself. Some within group percentages do not total 100 due to rounding.

[a] The type of households (male sole earner, female sole earner, and dual-earner) reflects the employment status of both household members at a particular point in time. Therefore, it is not surprising that we observe a portion of retirement savings contributions from the non-working spouse, which could reflect his or her labor force participation in prior years.

[b] Includes the balance of all defined contribution, IRA (Roth, regular, and rollover), and Keogh accounts held by all members of the primary economic unit, as defined by the Survey of Consumer Finances.

APPENDIX II: SELECTED SOCIAL SECURITY POLICY OPTIONS THAT MAY OFFSET EFFECTS OF CHANGES IN MARITAL PATTERNS

This appendix provides a summary of Social Security policy options, suggested by experts and cited in past GAO reports, to improve the retirement security of vulnerable populations.[1]

The options listed are not intended to be exhaustive, and each selected policy option may include multiple proposals.

In this report, we are not recommending or endorsing the adoption of any particular policy option.

Rather, we identify them as potential options for policymakers to consider, along with other relevant proposals, as they address retirement security issues. Table 8 presents options that focus specifically on modifying benefits for spouses and survivors.

Table 9 presents other options that would affect broader populations of vulnerable individuals, including those who do not qualify for spousal or survivor benefits, such as the never-married.

Table 8. Selected Policy Options That Target Spouses and Survivors

Selected policy options	Reduce the minimum marriage duration required for divorced spouse and survivor benefits	Increase spousal benefits for divorced spouses	Increase survivor benefits	Reduce spousal benefits & increase survivor benefits	Increase benefits for disabled surviving spouses	Adopt earnings sharing
See GAO reports	GAO-, GAO-10-101R, GAO-12-699	GAO-	GAO-, GAO-10-101R, GAO-12-699	GAO-	GAO-	GAO-
Targeted group	This option targets divorced spouses whose marriages lasted less than 10 years and therefore do not qualify for divorced spouse and survivor benefits.	This option targets divorced spouses who were married for at least 10 years and who qualify for divorced spouse and survivor benefits.	This option targets widow(er)s.	This option targets widow(er)s.	This option targets disabled surviving spouses.	This option targets divorced spouses whose marriages lasted less than 10 years and therefore do not qualify for spouse or survivor benefits, and whose incomes while married were lower than their spouses. An earnings sharing approach is often proposed as an alternative to existingspousal and survivor benefits.

Selected policy options	Reduce the minimum marriage duration required for divorced spouse and survivor benefits	Increase spousal benefits for divorced spouses	Increase survivor benefits	Reduce spousal benefits & increase survivor benefits	Increase benefits for disabled surviving spouses	Adopt earnings sharing
What happens now	Currently, a divorced spouse can receive benefits based on a retired worker's earnings record if the marriage lasted at least 10 years.	Currently, divorced spouses who qualify for spousal benefits receive a benefit equal to up to 50 percent of the worker's benefits. Divorced spouses who qualify for widow/widower benefits receive a benefit of up to 100 percent of the deceased worker's benefits.	Currently, a surviving spouse at full retirement age or older typically receives 100 percent of the worker's basic benefit amount. This decreases household income upon the death of one spouse by about one-third if the couple's retirement benefits had been based on one spouse's work history, and up to 50 percent if both spouses had been receiving retired worker benefits.	Currently, a surviving spouse at full retirement age or older typically receives 100 percent of the worker's basic benefit amount. This decreases household income upon the death of one spouse by about one-third if the couple's retirement benefits had been based on one spouse's work history and up to 50 percent if both spouses had been receiving retired worker benefits.	Currently, to qualify for disabled surviving spouse benefits, disabled surviving spouses must be at least age 50 and have become disabled not later than 7 years after the spouse's death or 7 years after last being eligible for mothers or father's benefits or widow(er)'s benefits based upon a disability. In addition, disabled surviving spouses younger than the full retirement age generally receive lower benefits than those who wait to receive their	Under the current system, a spouse who has not worked or who has low earnings can be entitled to a benefit equal to as much as one-half of the retired worker's full benefit. The total benefit received by the couple would be 150 percent of the worker's benefit. If the spouse is divorced, he or she can still get benefits based on a retired worker's earnings record if the marriage lasted at least 10 years, and the spouseis unmarried and at least 62 years old.

Table 8. (Continued)

Selected policy options	Reduce the minimum marriage duration required for divorced spouse and survivor benefits	Increase spousal benefits for divorced spouses	Increase survivor benefits	Reduce spousal benefits & increase survivor benefits	Increase benefits for disabled surviving spouses	Adopt earnings sharing
				Dual-earner couples experience a proportionally greater decrease in benefits upon the death of a spouse than single-earner couples experience. Researchers have expressed concern about whether this decline in total household benefits is too large to maintain the survivor's previous standard of living.	benefits until the full retirement age.	

Selected policy options	Reduce the minimum marriage duration required for divorced spouse and survivor benefits	Increase spousal benefits for divorced spouses	Increase survivor benefits	Reduce spousal benefits & increase survivor benefits	Increase benefits for disabled surviving spouses	Adopt earnings sharing
Selected reform options	Experts have recommended expanding eligibility for divorced spousal benefits to require a minimum of 7 years of marriage. Additionally, some experts have suggested marriage years could also be accumulated across multiple marriages. One Social Security reform proposal suggests that reducing the required marriage duration could be combined with a minimum work requirement for the divorced spouse.	Experts have suggested raising benefits for divorced spouses to 75 percent of the former spouse's benefit while the former spouse is still alive. Upon the death of the former spouse, the surviving divorced spouse would receive the full widow(er)'s benefit of 100 percent.	Experts have proposed calculating this new benefit in different ways. For example, the surviving spouse could receive 75 percent of the couple's retired-workers benefit but the benefit would be capped at the maximum earner's benefit or at the benefit of the "lifelong average earner." This option could also be targeted specifically toward low-income survivors, for example, by including a cap.	Some experts have proposed an increase in survivor benefits be paired with a decrease in spousal benefits, from one-half the retired worker's benefit to one-third.	Experts have proposed raising benefits for disabled surviving spouses to 100 percent of the deceased spouse's benefit. It would also remove the 7 year limitation and the age 50 requirement. Lastly, it would make divorced spouses who are disabled eligible for benefits on the same basis as disabled surviving spouses.	Earnings sharing, as proposed by experts, would combine married individuals' annual earnings and evenly divide them between the two spouses for each yearof marriage when calculating individuals' Social Security retirement benefits. Each spousewould accrue an individual benefit, even if only one of them worked. Divorced spouses whose marriages lasted less than 10 years would be entitled to the individual benefits accrued during the marriage.

Table 8. (Continued)

Selected policy options	Reduce the minimum marriage duration required for divorced spouse and survivor benefits	Increase spousal benefits for divorced spouses	Increase survivor benefits	Reduce spousal benefits & increase survivor benefits	Increase benefits for disabled surviving spouses	Adopt earnings sharing
	Combining at least 7 years of marriage with a minimum of 3 years of work would mimic the standard 10-year work requirement for Social Security retirement benefits.					This option is also seen as a way to equalize benefits received by dual-earner married couples with those of single-earner couples.
Some potential effects on the elderly	More divorced elderly would qualify for spousal benefits. For example, one study estimated that lowering the marriage-duration requirement from 10 to 7 years would increase benefits for about 8 percent of all divorced women age 62 and over in the year 2030.	Divorce can result in a substantial loss of assets and income. Some experts argue that a 50 percent benefit is not enough to keep divorced spouses from falling into poverty. It has been estimated that increasing the benefit rate	Increasing survivor benefits could help widow(er)s maintain their standard of living. However this option would not address benefit adequacy for those who do not qualify for spousal or survivor benefits.	Increasing survivor benefits could help widow(er)s maintain their standard of living. It would also smooth household benefit levels before and after widowhood. However, decreasing spousal benefits could have a negative impact on the couple while both spouses are	This option would increase benefits for a very vulnerable population. Both divorce and widowhood can result in a decrease in retirement security. Further, disabled surviving spouses, including those who have been divorced, cannot work and may have no partner	Earnings sharing could increase benefits for divorced elderly. However, this option would not do much to improve benefits for economically vulnerable beneficiaries, in part, because it is not well targeted. For example, SSA's simulations found thatearnings sharing would decrease benefits for the

Selected policy options	Reduce the minimum marriage duration required for divorced spouse and survivor benefits	Increase spousal benefits for divorced spouses	Increase survivor benefits	Reduce spousal benefits & increase survivor benefits	Increase benefits for disabled surviving spouses	Adopt earnings sharing
	Proponents of this option note that reducing the marriage requirement from 10 to 7 years would reflect current trends for shorter marriages. However, this option could benefit higher-income elderly who are not economically vulnerable.	for divorced spouses to 75 percent would lower the poverty rate among divorced spouses from 30 percent to 11 percent.		alive and would not address benefit adequacy for those who do not qualify for spousal or survivor benefits.	to depend on for support. In addition, disability issues affect a high number of divorced spouses, making them more vulnerable to income insecurity. One study estimated that more than one-fifth of all divorced spouses had health problems that meet disability criteria established by SSA.	majority of future retirees, although benefits for some would increase.
Other possible implications	The extent to which this option would increase Social Security costs depends on how many people would become eligible	This benefit increase would increase costs, thereby decreasing solvency.	Increasing benefits would increase costs and decrease solvency.	This option could provide savings to the Social Security system to partially or fully offset the costs of the increased survivor benefits.	This benefit increase would decrease solvency because it would increase costs. See above.	Because earnings sharing would increase benefits for some but decrease them for others, its net impact on Social Security's solvency is unclear.

Table 8. (Continued)

Selected policy options	Reduce the minimum marriage duration required for divorced spouse and survivor benefits	Increase spousal benefits for divorced spouses	Increase survivor benefits	Reduce spousal benefits & increase survivor benefits	Increase benefits for disabled surviving spouses	Adopt earnings sharing
	with a shorter marriage requirement and the way the option is designed. For example, not including a corresponding work requirement would increase costs more because people who have no work history would also be eligible.		The extent to which this option increases costs depends on how much greater the benefit amount is across all eligible survivors. Capping the amount of the increase based on income could help limit costs. This option could also be complex to administer, in part because it uses a "couple's benefit" as a baseline for calculating survivor benefits.			The extent towhich this option increases SSA's workload depends on the number of newly-eligible people who would receive benefits. Some additional administrative effort and cost would also be required to transition from the current system's spousal benefit to an earnings sharing approach, in part because of the need to verify marriage anddivorce data.

Selected policy options	Reduce the minimum marriage duration required for divorced spouse and survivor benefits	Increase spousal benefits for divorced spouses	Increase survivor benefits	Reduce spousal benefits & increase survivor benefits	Increase benefits for disabled surviving spouses	Adopt earnings sharing
			Since such a benefit does not currently exist in the Social Security system this could be problematic, for example, in cases where one of the spouses dies before retiring. In addition, there are many complicated rules for survivors because of an existing provision, called the widow(er)'s limit, that caps benefit amounts for some survivors. Benefit increases expected under this option could be negated by this provision.			

Source: GAO analysis of prior GAO reports.

Table 9. Selected Policy Options That Target All Elderly, Regardless of Marital Status

Selected policy options	Increase the minimum benefit	Provide caregiver credits	Reduce work requirements for eligibility	Supplement benefits for low-income single workers	Provide an additional Social Security benefit to the oldest old
See GAO reports	GAO-, GAO-10-101R, GAO-12-699	GAO-, GAO-10-101R, GAO-12-699	GAO-	GAO-	GAO-, GAO-12-699
Targeted group	The guaranteed minimum benefit option targets lifetime low earners.	Caregiver credits seek to improve benefit adequacy for workers, primarily women, who have shorter earnings records because they spent time providing care for children or elderly relatives and do not qualify for spousal benefits.	This option targets workers with low lifetime earnings due to short work histories, as opposed to those with long histories of low earnings.	This option targets low-income workers who never married or were not married long enough to qualify for spousal benefits.	Providing longevity insurance targets theoldest Social Security beneficiaries.
What happens now	A "special minimum" benefit provision was enacted in 1972 for workers with 11 or more covered years of employment.	Under the current system, Social Security eligibility and benefit amounts for retired workers depend on the amount of time a worker spends in covered employment.	Under current law, workers generally must accrue 40 credits—about 10 years of earnings—in covered employment to be eligible for Social Security retirement benefits based on their own work record.	In 2009, the benefit formula replaced 90 percent of the first $744 of a worker's average indexed monthly earnings (AIME), 32 percent of the AIME between $745 and $4,483, and 15 percent of the AIME above $4,483, up to a cap.	As people grow older, they risk outliving their other resources, become less able to work, and become more dependent on Social Security benefits for their income.
Selected policy	Increase the minimum	Provide caregiver	Reduce work	Supplement benefits for	Provide an additional

options	benefit	credits	requirements for eligibility	low-income single workers	Social Security benefit to the oldest old
	However, because the minimum benefit amount has not kept pace with wage growth, few people still qualify for the benefit. For workers not eligible for the special minimum benefit, benefits are generally calculated on the basis of a worker's average indexed monthly earnings during the 35 years in which they were the highest. While the benefit structure is progressive, a lifetime minimum- or low-wage worker would still have correspondingly low benefits.	Time spent out of covered employment as a caregiver may reduce benefits for workers, and others may not work enough to earn the required 40 credits generally required to be eligible for benefits.		A worker's AIME is calculated based on a worker's highest 35 years' earnings, after earnings have been indexed for wage growth over time.	While Social Security benefits are intendedto replace lost wages and are adjusted annually to reflect price inflation, they are not meant to be the sole sourceof retirement income. However, the value of other income sources, such as pensions and annuities, may be eroded by inflation over time.

Table 9. (Continued)

Selected policy options	Increase the minimum benefit	Provide caregiver credits	Reduce work requirements for eligibility	Supplement benefits for low-income single workers	Provide an additional Social Security benefit to the oldest old
	The current benefit formula does not distinguish between low average wages caused by low lifetime earnings or low average wages caused by years of unemployment.				
Selected reform options	Experts have suggested several options for increasing the minimum benefit. The amount and structure of the benefit varies among proposals, but most minimum benefit options are designed to address benefit adequacy by providing a retirement benefit	Experts have suggested a caregiver credit option, which can be designed in different ways. One design allows a specified amount of caregiving time, such as 3 or 4 years, to count as covered employment, and assigns a wage to that time.	Experts have suggested reducing the work requirements for Social Security retirement benefit eligibility, which would enable people who have shorter earnings histories to receive benefits. Benefit amounts would be calculated under the existing formula, which uses the worker's average indexed monthly earnings during the 35 years in which he or she earned the most,	Experts have suggested supplementing benefits for low-income single workers by adjusting the formula used to calculate Social Security retirement benefits. In one proposal, the first threshold in the benefit formula would be adjusted or supplemented so that it increased by one-half, from $744 to $1,116 in 2009, for eligible beneficiaries.	Experts have suggested that providing longevity insurance addresses concerns about benefit adequacy by increasing Social Security retirement benefits for beneficiaries who reach an advanced age. For example, Social Security recipients over the age of 80 or 85 could receive an additional benefit, such as an extra 5 percent on top of their regular benefit.

Selected policy options	Increase the minimum benefit	Provide caregiver credits	Reduce work requirements for eligibility	Supplement benefits for low-income single workers	Provide an additional Social Security benefit to the oldest old
	equal to some multiple of the federal poverty level, with the multiple based on years worked in covered employment. For example, one option would provide a minimum benefit equal to 120 percent of the federal poverty level for a minimum-wage earner who had worked for 30 years. Another option would provide a minimum benefit equal to 100 percent of the federal poverty level for a 30-year worker and 111 percent of the poverty level for a 40-year worker.	For example, an average wage for all workers could be assigned or a wage linked to an individual beneficiary's prior earnings could be used. Another design would exclude a limited number of caregiving years from the benefit calculation so that instead of averaging earnings over 35 years, earnings would be averaged over fewer years. A final design supplements caregivers' retired worker benefits directly, regardless of whether they took time out of the workforce for caregiving.	even if there were no earnings from covered employment during some of those years.	The benefit amount would be capped to prevent eligible workers from receiving higher benefits than those who just miss qualifying for the supplement. To be eligible for the supplement, a worker's AIME must be lower than a multiple of the existing formula's first threshold, such as 150 percent or 300 percent. For example, if the multiple were set at 300 percent, a worker whose AIME was less than $2,232 (3 x $744) in 2009 would qualify. To receive the supplement, a worker must have at least 30 years of covered employment and the worker cannot be eligible for spousal benefits, nor can anyone else claim spousal benefits based on that worker's earnings record.	Longevity insurance seeks to reduce the risk that the very old fall into poverty by increasing their Social Security benefits. This option could be targeted specifically toward low-income beneficiaries, or provided to all those who reach an advanced age. Work history could be an additional condition for eligibility.

Table 9. (Continued)

Selected policy options	Increase the minimum benefit	Provide caregiver credits	Reduce work requirements for eligibility	Supplement benefits for low-income single workers	Provide an additional Social Security benefit to the oldest old
		For example, an income-tested supplement could be given to increase retired worker benefits by 75 percent for those who have one child and 80 percent for those with two or more children. Both parents of a child would be eligible for this supplement, as long as the total household income did not exceed 125 percent of the federal poverty level.			For example, one longevity insurance proposal would increase benefits for people who have lowbenefits at age 82 and have at least 20 years of covered employment. It would provide a minimum benefit equal to 70 percent of the federal poverty level for a 20-year worker and increases the benefit for each additional year of work. Another proposal would increase benefits by 10 percent at age 85 for 30-year workers whose benefits are lower than 75 percent of the average benefit all workers receive.

Selected policy options	Increase the minimum benefit	Provide caregiver credits	Reduce work requirements for eligibility	Supplement benefits for low-income single workers	Provide an additional Social Security benefit to the oldest old
Some potential effects on the elderly	A guaranteed minimum benefit could help keep more elderly, lifetime low-earners out of poverty by increasing their monthly income. However, it is difficult to target lifetime low earners effectively. For example, requiring a long work history is problematic because low earners often have recurring periods of unemployment and cannot satisfy such a requirement. Thus, the target population may not be reached if a lifetime of work is required to earn the benefit. However, if a lifetime of work is not required, some people outside the target population would also benefit, e.g.,	Caregiver credits seek to improve benefit adequacy for workers, primarily women, who have shorter earnings records because they spent time providing care for children or elderly relatives and do not qualify for spousal benefits because they never married or were not married long enough to qualify for them. For various reasons, implementing this option may not reach the target population. For example, low-income people are less likely to be able to take time off from work.	Reducing the Social Security work requirement is an option that targets workers with low lifetime earnings due to short work histories, as opposed to those with long histories of low earnings. According to SSA officials, many people fall just short of the 40 credits requirement because they have intermittent work histories. However, officials also said many of those people may already be eligible for spousal benefits, resulting in few people benefiting from this option. In addition, agency officials and experts said benefits based on such short work histories are likely to be very low and questioned the effectiveness of this option in addressing benefit adequacy.	The benefit supplement option targets lifetime low earners who never married or were not married long enough to qualify for spousal benefits. Low-income single and divorced women are expected to benefit most from this option.	Women, who tend to live longer than men,would be more likely to receive this extra benefit. Older women may need extra benefits as income and assets may have been usedto care for a deceased spouse or to pay for increasing medical costs. An additional benefit may be particularly helpful for low-income women. While this could be an effective option for addressing concerns about benefit adequacy for the very old, unless this option is specifically targeted toward low-income beneficiaries, most of the benefits would accrue to higher-income people because they tend tolive longer.

Table 9. (Continued)

Selected policy options	Increase the minimum benefit	Provide caregiver credits	Reduce work requirements for eligibility	Supplement benefits for low-income single workers	Provide an additional Social Security benefit to the oldest old
	higher-wage workers who worked for a short period of time.	Therefore, people who have relatively higher incomes may benefit more from the creation of caregiver credits.			In addition, this option could create disincentives to savefor retirement or incentives to spend down resources before beneficiaries become old enough to qualify for the longevity increase.
Other possible implications	Cost implications of this option depend on the number of work years required for eligibility, since that requirement will directly influence the number of people who would qualify for benefit increases. A shorter work requirement will result in more people being eligible, and thus costs will be higher.	Because caregiver credits increase benefits, they have cost implications for Social Security's solvency. The extent to which this option affects solvency depends largely on who would be eligible to receive the credit: one or both parents, all caregivers, or just those who have low incomes.	Because this option increases the number of people receiving benefits, it has cost implications for Social Security's solvency. The number of credits required will directly influence the number of people who would be newly eligible for benefits. A shorter work requirement will result in more people being eligible.	The extent to which this option would decrease Social Security's solvency would depend largely on the number of people who would be eligible for it. A key factor that directly influences the number of eligible beneficiaries is the multiple that would be applied to a worker's AIME, ranging from 150 percent to 300 percent. Another factor that could influence cost is the way "single" is defined for purposes of determining eligibility.	Providing longevity insurance would increase Social Security program costs. Key factors that influence costs include the age at which the benefit increases, the amount of the increase, and whether all beneficiaries or only low-income ones are eligible to receive the benefit. In addition, costs could increase if life expectancy continues to increase in the future.

Selected policy options	Increase the minimum benefit	Provide caregiver credits	Reduce work requirements for eligibility	Supplement benefits for low-income single workers	Provide an additional Social Security benefit to the oldest old
	Additionally, the multiple of the federal poverty level used can have a significant impact on cost.	Extending eligibility to a greater number of people will increase costs. In addition, the number of years that credits may be received and the wage assigned to those years will impact costs. Caregiver credits would be complex to administer. A key issue is how to verify that care was provided to a qualifying person. While a birth certificate could be used to document child care, elder care would be more burdensome to document. Measuring time off and verifying that caregiving actually occurred would also be difficult.	However, because few people are actually expected to receive benefits under this option, and those who do are expected to receive modest benefits, the impact of a reduced work requirement on program solvency is unlikely to be very large. Furthermore, because few people are expected to gain eligibility under this option, the impact on SSA's workload is likely to be small.	Moreover, determining an individual's single status could be administratively complex because people's marital statuses change over time and could change after an initial determination is made, for example, from single to married.	While this option would be easy to administer, adding measures to improvetargeting would increase administrative complexity.

Source: GAO analysis of prior GAO reports.

End Notes

[1] Relevant federal laws governing these benefits include the Social Security Act, which governs the Social Security Old-Age and Survivors Insurance program (referred to in this report as Social Security retirement benefits), as well as the Employee Retirement Income Security Act of 1974 (ERISA) and the Internal Revenue Code (IRC), which govern certain employer-sponsored pension plans.

[2] DB plans typically offer retirement benefits to a retiree in the form of an annuity that provides a monthly payment for life, the value of which is typically determined by a formula based on particular factors specified by the plan, such as salary or years of service. ERISA generally requires that covered DB plans pay benefits in the form of a qualified joint and survivor annuity (QJSA), unless certain waiver requirements are met, including the spouse's written consent.

[3] Under DC plans, such as 401(k) plans, workers and employers may make contributions to individual accounts. In contrast to DB plans, DC plans are not generally required to offer a lifetime annuity and DC plans more often provide participants with a lump sum distribution as the only option.

[4] The analysis of the restricted SIPP data was made possible through the use of the SIPP Synthetic Beta data, which was funded by the Census Bureau and SSA, with additional funding from NSF Grants #0427889 and #0339191. The Synthetic Data Server is funded through NSF grant SES-1042181.

[5] Because these data sources are probability samples, our results based on these data sources are estimates and subject to sampling error. In this report, sampling errors for estimates are presented along with their associated margins of error at the 95% confidence level. With the exception of the MINT projections, for which SSA does not typically produce confidence intervals, any differences between point estimates discussed in this report are statistically significant at the 95% confidence level unless otherwise noted. Please refer to appendix I for additional information on sampling error.

[6] For additional details on our scope and methods, see appendix I.

[7] Carmen DeNavas-Walt, Bernadette D. Proctor, and Jessica C. Smith, U. S. Census Bureau, *Income, Poverty, and Health Insurance Coverage in the United States: 2012*, Current Population Reports, P60-245 (Washington, D.C.: September 2013).

[8] See Karen C. Holden and Angela Fontes, "Economic Security in Retirement: How Changes in Employment and Marriage Have Altered Retirement-Related Economic Risks for Women," *Journal of Women, Politics, & Policy,* vol. 30 (2009), 173-197.

[9] Under the Internal Revenue Code, the federal income tax liability of a married couple may not be the same as that of two similarly-situated single taxpayers. Depending on the circumstances, there could be either a marriage penalty (married couple owes more tax) or a marriage bonus (married couple owes less tax).

[10] This report focuses on the retirement income of private sector workers and their spouses; the retirement income of public sector (federal, state, and local government) workers was beyond the scope of this review.

[11] See generally 42 U.S.C. § 401 *et seq.*

[12] Social Security spousal and survivor benefits may be offset in certain circumstances due to the Social Security Windfall Elimination Provision or the Government Pension Offset. For more information on these provisions, see GAO, *Opportunities to Reduce Potential Duplication in Government Programs, Save Tax Dollars, and Enhance Revenue*, GAO-11-318SP (Washington, D.C.: March 1, 2011).

[13] See 29 U.S.C. § 1055.

[14] See Michael J. Brien and Constantijn W.A. Panis, *Annuities in the Context of Defined Contribution Plans*, a study prepared for the U.S. Department of Labor, November 2011. In some limited circumstances, DC plans may be required to offer a QJSA or QPSA. 29 U.S.C. § 1055(b)(1)(B)-(C).

[15] See 26 U.S.C. § 408.

[16] United States v. Windsor, 133 S. Ct. 2675 (2013).

[17] For example, on September 18, 2013, the Department of Labor issued guidance explaining its interpretation of the definitions of "spouse" and "marriage" under ERISA, in light of the U.S. Supreme Court decision. See Technical Release No. 2013-04. On August 29, 2013, the Department of the Treasury and the IRS ruled that same-sex couples, legally married in jurisdictions that recognize their marriages, will be treated as married for federal tax purposes. The ruling applies regardless of whether the couple lives in a jurisdiction that recognizes same-sex marriage or a jurisdiction that does not recognize same-sex marriage. Rev. Rul. 2013-17, 2013-38 I.R.B. 201. In addition, according to SSA officials, the agency is processing some types of claims for members of same-sex married couples and paying benefits when they are due. SSA is also working with the Department of Justice to develop and implement additional policies and processing instructions related to the *Windsor* decision.

[18] Craig Copeland, Retirement Plan Participation: Survey of Income and Program Participation (SIPP) Data, 2012, EBRI Notes, vol. 34, no. 8, Employee Benefit Research Institute (Washington, D.C.: August 2013).

[19] Sudipto Banerjee, "Annuity and Lump-Sum Decisions in Defined Benefit Plans: The Role of Plan Rules," EBRI Issue Brief, no. 381 (January 2013).

[20] JPMorgan Chase & Co., *Pension Pulse* (New York, N.Y.: Fall 2012).

[21] GAO, Unemployed Older Workers: Many Experience Challenges Regaining Employment and Face Reduced Retirement Security, GAO-12-445 (Washington, D.C.: Apr. 25, 2012).

[22] Despite the growth in the proportion of the divorced population, the divorce rate has actually leveled off in recent years. According to data from the National Center for Health Statistics, the annual divorce rate for married women increased from 15 to 20 divorces per 1,000 married women between 1970 and 1975 and remained at that level through the mid-1990s. However, for individuals 50 and older, the divorce rate between 1990 and 2010 more than doubled. See Rose M. Kreider and Renee Ellis, U.S. Census Bureau, *Number, Timing, and Duration of Marriages and Divorces: 2009*, Current Population Reports, Household Economic Studies, P70-125 (Washington, D.C.: May 2011), and Susan L. Brown and I-Fen Lin, "The Gray Divorce Revolution. Rising Divorce Among Middle-Aged and Older Adults, 1990-2010" *Journals of Gerontology Series B: Psychological Sciences and Social Sciences*, vol. 67 no. 6, 731-741 (2012).

[23] Casey E. Copen, Kimberly Daniels, and William D. Mosher, U.S. Department of Health and Human Services, Centers for Disease Control and Prevention, National Center for Health Statistics, "First Premarital Cohabitation in the United States: 2006-2010 National Survey of Family Growth," *National Health Statistics Reports*, Number 64 (Atlanta, GA: April 4, 2013).

[24] A federal interagency group, headed by the Office of Management and Budget, is investigating new methodologies for gathering and utilizing household relationship data in federal surveys, with a primary goal of improving statistics on same-sex couple households. While there is no established timetable, new question wording and survey formats are being assessed in large-scale field tests. If successful, they may be implemented more broadly.

[25] Unless otherwise noted, throughout this report individuals in the white, black, and Asian racial and ethnic categories are non-Hispanic.

[26] See appendix I for further details on the data and our analyses.

[27] While this report focuses on the effects of rising labor force participation among married women, policy analysts are increasingly concerned about the steady decline in men's labor force participation overall, which has been more pronounced among unmarried men in recent years.

[28] We obtained data for labor force participation rates among women with children of varying ages from the BLS report, *Women in the Labor Force: A Databook,* U.S. Bureau of Labor Statistics, Report 1040 (February 2013). This report presented data on labor force participation rates of mothers with children starting in 1975.

[29] Several legislative changes related to maternal employment may have played a role in the rising labor force participation of mothers in the 1970s through the 1990s. These included 1976 changes to the federal tax code that permitted working families with a dependent child to take a tax credit for child care costs, a 1978 amendment to Title VII of the Civil Rights Act of 1964 to prohibit sex discrimination on the basis of pregnancy or childbirth, and the Family and Medical Leave Act of 1993, which requires covered employers to provide, at minimum, up to 12 weeks of unpaid parental leave for eligible employees. See Lynda Laughlin, U.S. Census Bureau, "Maternity Leave and Employment Patterns of First-Time Mothers: 1961-2008," *Current Population Reports, Household Economic Studies*, P70-128 (October 2011).

[30] U.S. Bureau of Labor Statistics, *Women in the Labor Force: A Databook*, BLS Reports, Report 1040 (Washington, D.C.: February 2013).

[31] In addition to caring for children, many women also bear responsibility for caring for an elderly person or a disabled adult, which can affect women's participation in the workforce. Some researchers have argued that today's generation of middle-aged women faces a significant caretaking burden, providing financial and practical support for elderly parents at an age when many workers should be contributing heavily to their own retirement funds. Due to changes in the SIPP survey questions about caretaking responsibilities, we were unable to examine trends over time in the percentage of women who take time out from the workforce to care for elderly or disabled adults. However, our analysis of the 2008 SIPP shows that in 2008, approximately 5 percent of women age 50-62 had taken at least 6 months off of work to care for an elderly or disabled adult.

[32] Lynda Laughlin, U.S. Census Bureau, "Maternity Leave and Employment Patterns of First-Time Mothers: 1961-2008," *Current Population Reports, Household Economic Studies,* P70-128 (October 2011).

[33] This section primarily focuses on women's receipt of spousal benefits because only a small percentage of men (less than 1 percent as of 2012) currently receive Social Security spousal benefits. If women's wages continue to rise relative to men's, men's receipt of spousal benefits may rise in the future. See Objective 3 for further discussion of projected receipt of future benefits by sex and benefit type. All statistics in this section of the report pertaining to the Social Security beneficiary categories of spouse-only, dually-entitled spouse, widow-only, and dually-entitled widow include divorced spouses who are eligible for spousal and survivor benefits because they were married for at least 10 years.

[34] Howard M. Iams and Christopher R. Tamborini, "The Implications of Marital History Change on Women's Eligibility for Social Security Wife and Widow Benefits, 1990-2009," *Social Security Bulletin*, vol. 72, no. 2 (2012).

[35] ibid.

[36] Despite the high correlation between race, education and income, the differences in eligibility between blacks and other racial and ethnic categories persisted even after accounting for differences in income and education levels, according to our analysis of SIPP data.

[37] Here we are presenting data for women age 50-59 for comparability with the data reported by Iams et al. Similar trends are seen among women age 55-64. Among women age 55-64 in the lowest quintile of income, the percentage who were married or had been married for at least 10 years declined from an estimated 85 percent in 1996 to an estimated 73 percent in 2008. Among women age 55-64 in the highest quintile of income, the percentage who were married or had been married for at least 10 years declined from an estimated 97 to 95 percent.

[38] These estimates represent a lower bound of the number of women who have been in a marriage for at least 10 years. The SIPP marital history module provides the year in which each marriage starts and—for those marriages that have ended in death or divorce—the year in which each marriage terminates. Because the month of the marriage start / end date is not provided, the length of the marital spell is imprecise. For example, consider a person who married in the year 2000 and divorced in the year 2010. The estimated length of the marriage spell is 10 years. However, if the person married in the second half of the start year (say, December 2000) and divorced in the first half of the termination year (say January 2010), the actual length of the marriage spell would be less than 10 years – in this example, 9 years and two months. To avoid this problem, we defined a 10-year marriage as one in which the termination date minus the start date is at least 11 years. With this more conservative definition, we avoid including any marriages that fall short of 10 years—but we also exclude some marriages that are exactly 10 years. These estimates are therefore a lower bound of the number of people who have 10-year marriages.

[39] The lack of statistically significant differences may be the result of data limitations associated with the small sample size available in the SIPP Gold Standard Data. See appendix I for more details on our data and the analyses.

[40] Household DC plan and IRA assets include the balance of all defined contribution, IRA (Roth, traditional, and rollover), and Keogh accounts held by all members of the primary economic unit, as defined by the Survey of Consumer Finances. DB plans are not included in this measure of household savings.

[41] This finding is consistent with recent results by Irena Dushi and Howard Iams. Using SIPP data from 2009, they find that in households in which both spouses contributed to a DC plan, the wife's contribution comprised around 42 percent of the total family contribution. See Irena Dushi and Howard M. Iams, "Pension Plan Participation Among Married Couples," *Social Security Bulletin*, vol. 73, no. 3 (2013).

[42] The type of household (male sole earner, female sole earner, and dual-earner) reflects the employment status of both household members at a particular point in time. Therefore, it is not surprising that we observe a portion of retirement savings contributions from the non-working spouse, which could reflect their labor force participation in prior years.

[43] Due to limitations with our sample size, we expanded the analysis of individuals age 55- 64 to include individuals in households age 50-54. See appendix I for more details on our analyses and data limitations.

[44] For purposes of this section of the report, pension income is defined based on the structure of the SCF data on current benefits from pensions. Specifically it refers to any income from a pension—from a current or past job or a disability benefit—that is not an account plan, such as a 401(k) plan, where the participant can take the whole balance as one payment. In addition, a survivor benefit includes any type of spousal benefit provided after the

participant's death, regardless of the duration of the benefit received, amount of benefit received, or payment method (lump sum or annuity). Survivor benefits from tax-qualified defined benefit plans are required to be in the form of a qualified joint and survivor annuity, unless the participant (with the spouse's consent) chooses to receive an alternate form of benefit, such as a single life annuity. For the purposes of this report, due to limitations in the SCF data, a survivor benefit may also include households that have chosen to annuitize their defined contribution plan savings or households that are receiving an annuity from a divorce settlement under a qualified domestic relations order (QDRO). According to our estimates, between 2001 and 2010, the proportion of married households that opted out of a survivor benefit ranged from 35 to 44 percent. However, the differences over this period were not statistically significant.

[45] Typically, a joint and survivor annuity provides a smaller monthly payment while the participant is alive, to allow for payments to the spouse upon the participant's death. A single life annuity can provide a higher monthly payment because it lasts only for the life of the participant.

[46] This finding was significant at the 90 percent confidence level. These results were generally consistent with what has been found in past work by outside researchers. See, for example, Richard W. Johnson, Cori E. Uccello, and Joshua H. Goldwyn, "Who Forgoes Survivor Protection in Employer-Sponsored Pension Annuities?" *The Gerontologist*, vol. 45, no 1, 26-35 (2005).

[47] This section primarily focuses on women's receipt of spousal benefits because only a small percentage of men (less than 1 percent as of 2012) currently receive Social Security spousal benefits. If women's wages continue to rise relative to men's, men's receipt of spousal benefits may rise in the future. Additionally, the Social Security benefit projections presented in this report are based on a model that was developed prior to the U.S. Supreme Court's June 2013 decision holding a provision of the Defense of Marriage Act to be unconstitutional. See *United States v. Windsor*, 133 S. Ct. 2675 (2013). Consequently, the estimates are based on heterosexual marriages exclusively and do not incorporate trends among same-sex married couples.

[48] Barbara A. Butrica and Karen E. Smith, "The Retirement Prospects of Divorced Women", *Social Security Bulletin*, vol. 72, no. 1 (2012).

[49] Rose M. Kreider and Renee Ellis, U.S. Census Bureau, *Number, Timing, and Duration of Marriages and Divorces: 2009*, Current Population Reports, Household Economic Studies, P70-125, (Washington, D.C.: May 2011).

[50] The overall labor force participation rate is actually projected to decline gradually for both men and women. According to the U.S. Bureau of Labor Statistics, women's labor force participation is expected to decline from its peak of 60 percent in 1999 to 53 percent in 2040. Men's labor force participation is expected to fall to 64.8 percent in 2040. See U.S. Bureau of Labor Statistics, *Women in the Labor Force: A Databook*, Report 1040 (Washington, D.C.: February 2013) for historical data. The U.S. Bureau of Labor Statistics provided the 2040 projected data to GAO in a separate analysis. However, the pay gap between men and women is also expected to continue to narrow, further decreasing the gap between women's and men's lifetime earnings. For example, according to projections by the Center for Retirement Research, wives born from 1966 to 1975 are expected to earn about 68 percent of their husbands' earnings, more than double the ratio for wives born from 1931 to 1935. See April Yanyuan Wu, Nadia S. Karamcheva, Alicia H. Munnell, and Patrick Purcell, "How Does Women Working Affect Social Security Replacement Rates?"

Center for Retirement Research at Boston College, *Issue in Brief*, no. 13-10 (Chestnut Hill, MA: June 2013).

[51] For all Social Security beneficiary projections in this section of the report, the categories of spouse-only, dually-entitled spouse, widow(er)-only, and dually-entitled widow(er) include divorced spouses who are eligible for spousal and survivor benefits because they were married for at least 10 years.

[52] See Barbara A. Butrica and Karen E. Smith, "The Impact of Changes in Couples' Earnings on Married Women's Social Security Benefits," *Social Security Bulletin*, vol. 72, no. 1 (2012). However, as explained in greater detail below, as couples' earnings become more similar, the Social Security survivor benefit replaces a smaller proportion of the couples' Social Security income received by the household when both spouses were alive.

[53] There are no substantial differences by race in the type of benefits men received in 2012 or are projected to receive in 2040.

[54] For example, the median household income in 2010 for women 65 and older was $27,610 for black women, $32,820 for Hispanic women, $33,590 for white women, and $41,960 for Asian women. For men the incomes ranged from $35,310 for black men to $47,530 for Asian men. See *GAO, Retirement Security: Women Still Face Challenges*, GAO-12-699 (Washington, D.C.: July 19, 2012).

[55] The median household income in 2010 for married women 65 and older was $46,990. The next highest income level for women was $25,320, for divorced women. For married men the median income was $49,720 and the next highest level was $35,080 for separated men. See GAO-12-699.

[56] The preretirement income used in this example is the annual equivalent of the average indexed monthly earnings used to calculate Social Security benefits.

[57] In general, the widow(er) of a retired worker is eligible to receive a survivor benefit that equals 100% of the deceased retired worker's benefit amount, assuming that the widow(er) claims this benefit at the full retirement age—which varies depending on the worker's date of birth. Widow(er)s may claim benefits as early as age 60, although the amount is reduced accordingly.

[58] DeNavas-Walt et al., Income, Poverty, and Health Insurance Coverage.

[59] Barbara A. Butrica and Karen E. Smith, "The Impact of Changes in Couples' Earnings on Married Women's Social Security Benefits," *Social Security Bulletin*, vol. 72, no. 1 (2012).

[60] GAO previously reported on this topic in GAO, *Social Security: Issues Involving Benefit Equity for Working Women*, GAO/HEHS-96-55 (Washington, D.C.: Apr. 10, 1996).

[61] Appendix II provides a detailed summary of these policy options. We reviewed GAO's prior work and selected these options from among a larger list of policy options presented in three prior GAO reports. We selected these policy options based on either their specific focus on spousal or survivor benefits or their broader focus on elderly populations that are vulnerable to poverty. See also GAO-12-699; GAO, *Social Security: Options to Protect Benefits for Vulnerable Groups When Addressing Program Solvency*, GAO-10-101R (Washington, D.C.: Dec. 7, 2009); and GAO, *Retirement Security: Women Face Challenges in Ensuring Financial Security in Retirement*, GAO-08-105 (Washington, D.C.: Oct. 11, 2007). The listed options are not intended to be exhaustive. In this report, we are not recommending or endorsing the adoption of any particular policy option. Rather, we identify them as potential options for policymakers to consider, along with other relevant proposals, as they address retirement security issues.

[62] The current maximum of 67 percent applies to the survivor of a couple that had previously received a retired-worker benefit plus spouse-only or plus a dually-entitled spouse benefit,

i.e., 150 percent of the retired worker's benefit. Upon the death of one spouse, the surviving spouse receives 100 percent of the retired-worker benefit, which equals 67 percent of the prior total household benefit. As an example, see the one-earner couple in figure 20 above.

[63] The Special Minimum Primary Insurance Amount provision was added by the Social Security Amendments of 1972, Pub. L. No. 92-603, § 101, 86 Stat. 1329, 1333-35 (codified as amended at 42 U.S.C. § 415(a)(1)(C)(i)).

[64] Currently, fewer beneficiaries qualify for the Special Minimum Benefit every year because it is indexed to price inflation, which has risen less than regular initial Social Security benefits, which are indexed to wage inflation. As a result, the Special Minimum Benefit does not necessarily ensure that individuals who have spent many years in Social Security-covered employment will have an income above the poverty line. As of 2012, the maximum possible Special Minimum Benefit was $9,487 annually. In 2012, the federal poverty guideline was $11,170 for a single person. See Alison M. Shelton, Congressional Research Service, *Social Security: The Minimum Benefit Provision*, R41518 (Washington, D.C.: May 24, 2012).

[65] Copeland, "Retirement Plan Participation".

[66] We identified these policy options for DB and DC plans through interviews and consultations with retirement policy experts representing a range of perspectives and from different types of organizations including government, academia, advocacy groups, and the private sector. The listed options are not intended to be exhaustive and we are not recommending or endorsing the adoption of any particular policy option. Rather, we identify them as potential options for policymakers to consider, along with other relevant proposals, as they address retirement security issues.

[67] In order to help ease the administrative burden of documenting spousal consent in DB plans, Internal Revenue Service regulations allow electronic acknowledgement or notarization but still require the signature of the spouse to be witnessed in the physical presence of the plan representative or notary public to avert coercion and fraud. However, one expert we interviewed believes that notaries have not yet begun using this method to document spousal consent because they have not yet found a viable way to implement it. See also GAO, *Private Pensions: Revised Electronic Disclosure Rules Could Broaden Use and Better Protect Participant Choice*, GAO-13-594 (Washington, D.C.: Sept. 13, 2013).

[68] However, while women are closing the pension gap and saving more for retirement, they still generally lag behind men. See GAO-12-699.

End Notes for Appendix I

[1] The analysis of the Gold Standard SIPP data was made possible through the use of the SIPP Synthetic Beta data, which was funded by the Census Bureau and the Social Security Administration (SSA), with additional funding from NSF Grants #0427889 and #0339191.The Synthetic Data Server is funded through National Science Foundation (NSF) grant SES-1042181.

[2] See Jess Bricker, et al., "Changes in U.S. Family Finances from 2007 to 2010: Evidence from the Survey of Consumer Finances," *Federal Reserve Bulletin,* vol. 98, no. 2 (June 2012).

[3] For more information on the MINT6, see Karen E. Smith, Melissa M. Favreault, Barbara A. Butrica, and Philip Issa, *Final Report: Modeling Income in the Near Term Version 6*, The Urban Institute (December 2010).

[4] An additional 1,091 of the 42,803 women in the SIPP data did not have SSNs. These women, however, did not have a birth date in the SIPP data, so we do not know what proportion of them were age 62 and over and might have been receiving Social Security benefits and therefore excluded from our analysis. To the extent that women who did not have SSNs differ systematically from women included in the analysis, this represents a potential source of bias.

[5] GAO, *Retirement Security: Women Still Face Challenges*, GAO-12-699 (Washington, D.C.: July 2012).

[6] See GAO, Retirement Security: Women Still Face Challenges, GAO-12-699 (Washington, D.C.: July 2012); GAO, Social Security: Options to Protect Benefits for Vulnerable Groups When Addressing Program Solvency, GAO-10-101R (Washington, D.C.: December 2009); and GAO, Retirement Security: Women Face Challenges in Ensuring Financial Security in Retirement, GAO-08-105 (Washington, D.C.: October 2007).

End Notes for Appendix II

[1] The policy options described in this appendix have been suggested by experts including agency officials and retirement security researchers and were compiled directly from prior GAO reports. For this report, we did not conduct an independent analysis of the possible legal effects of each policy option.

In: Marriage and Retirement Security
Editor: Ian M. Styles
ISBN: 978-1-63321-120-9
© 2014 Nova Science Publishers, Inc.

Chapter 2

SOCIAL SECURITY PRIMER*

Dawn Nuschler

SUMMARY

The Social Security program began in the 1930s and has been modified by Congress many times over the past seven decades. Today, Social Security provides monthly cash benefits to retired or disabled workers and their family members, and to the family members of deceased workers. Among the beneficiary population, approximately 81% are retired or disabled workers, and 19% are the family members of retired, disabled, or deceased workers. In November 2013, 57.9 million beneficiaries received a total of $67 billion in benefit payments for the month. The average benefit payment was $1,164.

Workers become eligible for Social Security benefits for themselves and their family members by working in Social Security-covered employment. An estimated 93% of workers in paid employment or self-employment are covered, and their earnings are subject to the Social Security payroll tax. In 2014, employers and employees each pay 6.2% of covered earnings, up to the annual limit on taxable earnings ($117,000 in 2014).

To be eligible for a Social Security retired-worker benefit, a person generally needs at least 40 earnings credits, or 10 years of Social Security-covered employment (among other requirements). Fewer earnings credits are needed for a disabled-worker benefit, depending on

---

* This is an edited, reformatted and augmented version of Congressional Research Service Publication, No. R42035, dated January 13, 2014.

the worker's age. A worker's initial monthly benefit is based on his or her career-average earnings in covered employment. Social Security retired-worker benefits are first payable at the age of 62, subject to a permanent reduction for early retirement. Full (or unreduced) retirement benefits are first payable at the full retirement age (FRA), which is increasing gradually from 65 to 67 under a law enacted by Congress in 1983. The FRA will reach 67 for persons born in 1960 or later (i.e., persons who become eligible for retirement benefits at the age of 62 in 2022 or later).

In addition to payroll taxes, Social Security is financed by federal income taxes that some beneficiaries pay on a portion of their benefits and by interest income that is earned on the Treasury securities held by the Social Security trust funds. In 2012, the Social Security trust funds had receipts totaling $840 billion, expenditures totaling $786 billion, and accumulated assets (in the form of Treasury securities) totaling $2.7 trillion. Projections by the Social Security Board of Trustees show that, based on the program's current financing and benefit structure, benefits scheduled under current law can be paid in full and on time until 2033. The projections also show that Social Security expenditures will exceed income by about 20% *on average* over the next 75 years. Restoring long-range trust fund solvency and other policy objectives have made Social Security reform an issue of ongoing congressional interest and debate.

This report provides an overview of Social Security financing and benefits under current law. Specifically, the report covers the origins and a brief history of the program; Social Security financing and the status of the trust funds; how Social Security benefits are computed; the types of Social Security benefits available to workers and their family members; the basic eligibility requirements for each type of benefit; the scheduled increase in the Social Security retirement age enacted in 1983; and the federal income taxation of Social Security benefits.

INTRODUCTION

Social Security is a primarily self-financed program that provides monthly cash benefits to retired or disabled workers and their family members and to the family members of deceased workers. As of November 2013, there were 57.9 million Social Security beneficiaries. Of those, 40.7 million (70.4%) were retired workers and family members, 11.0 million (19.0%) were disabled workers and family members, and 6.2 million (10.7%) were survivors of deceased workers.[1]

Social Security is financed primarily by payroll taxes paid by covered workers and their employers. An estimated 164.9 million workers are covered by Social Security.[2] Employers and employees each pay 6.2% of covered earnings, up to the annual limit on taxable earnings ($117,000 in 2014);[3] self-employed individuals pay 12.4% of net self-employment income, up to the annual limit ($117,000 in 2014).[4] Social Security is also credited with tax revenues from the federal income taxes paid by some beneficiaries on a portion of their benefits. In addition, Social Security receives interest income from Social Security trust fund investments. Social Security income and outgo are accounted for in two separate trust funds authorized under Title II of the Social Security Act: the Federal Old-Age and Survivors Insurance (OASI) trust fund and the Federal Disability Insurance (DI) trust fund.[5] In 2012, the combined Social Security trust funds (OASDI) had total receipts of $840 billion, total expenditures of $786 billion, and accumulated holdings (assets) of $2.7 trillion.[6]

Origins and Brief History of Social Security

Title II of the original Social Security Act of 1935[7] established a national plan designed to provide economic security for the nation's workers. The system of Old-Age Insurance it created provided benefits to individuals who were aged 65 or older and who had "earned" retirement benefits through work in jobs covered by the system. Benefits were to be financed by a payroll tax paid by employees and their employers on wages up to a base amount ($3,000 per year at the time). Monthly benefits were to be based on cumulative wages in covered jobs. The law related the amount of the benefit to the amount of a worker's wages covered by the program, but the formula was progressive. That is, the formula was weighted to replace a larger share of the earnings of low-wage workers compared with those of higher-wage workers. Before the Old-Age Insurance program was in full operation, the Social Security Amendments of 1939[8] shifted the emphasis of Social Security from protection of the individual worker to protection of the family by extending monthly cash benefits to the dependents and survivors of workers. The program now provided Old-Age and Survivors Insurance (OASI).

During the decades that followed, changes to the Social Security program were mainly ones of expansion. Coverage of workers became nearly universal (the largest groups remaining outside the system are state and local government employees who have not chosen to join the system and federal employees who were hired before 1984). In 1956, Congress established the Disability Insurance (DI) program.[9] Over the years, there were increases in the payroll tax rate, which increased from 2.0% of pay (1.0% each for employees and employers) in the 1937-1949 period to its current level of 12.4%.[10] In addition, there were increases in the amount of wages subject to the payroll tax (the taxable wage base), which increased from $3,000 in the 1937-1950 period to its current level of $117,000.[11] The types of individuals eligible for benefits were expanded over the years,[12] and benefit levels were increased periodically. In 1972, legislation provided for automatic cost-of-living adjustments, starting in 1975, indexed to the change in consumer prices as measured by the Consumer Price Index for Urban Wage Earners and Clerical Workers (CPI-W) published by the Department of Labor's Bureau of Labor Statistics.[13]

Beginning in the late 1970s, legislative action regarding Social Security became more concentrated on solving persistent financing problems. Legislation enacted in 1977 raised taxes and curtailed future benefit growth in an effort to shore up the system's finances.[14] Still, in 1982, the OASI trust fund needed to borrow assets from the DI trust fund and the Medicare Hospital Insurance (HI) trust fund (borrowed amounts were fully repaid by 1986). In 1983, Congress passed additional major legislation that was projected to restore solvency to the Social Security system *on average* over the 75-year projection period at that time.[15]

Current projections by the Social Security Board of Trustees show that the Social Security system has a long-range funding shortfall and that the system will operate with annual cash-flow deficits each year through the end of the 75-year projection period (2087). These projections, and other factors, have focused attention on potential Social Security program changes.[16]

SOCIAL SECURITY FINANCING

The Social Security program is financed primarily by revenues from Federal Insurance Contributions Act (FICA) taxes and Self Employment Contributions Act (SECA) taxes. FICA taxes are paid by both employers and employees, but it is employers who remit the taxes to the U.S. Treasury. Employers remit FICA taxes on a regular basis throughout the year (e.g., weekly, monthly, quarterly, or annually), depending on the employer's level of total employment taxes (Social Security, Medicare, and federal individual income tax withholding).

The FICA tax rate of 7.65% each for employers and employees has two components: 6.2% for Social Security and 1.45% for Medicare HI.[17] Under current law, employers and employees each pay 6.2% of covered wages, up to the taxable wage base, in Social Security payroll taxes. The SECA tax rate is

15.3% for self-employed individuals, with 12.4% for Social Security and 2.9% for Medicare HI. Self-employed individuals pay 12.4% of net self-employment income, up to the taxable wage base, in Social Security payroll taxes. One-half of the SECA taxes are allowed as a deduction for federal income tax purposes.[18] SECA taxes are normally paid once a year as part of filing an annual individual income tax return.[19]

In addition to Social Security payroll taxes, the Social Security program has two other sources of income. First, certain Social Security beneficiaries must include a portion of Social Security benefits in taxable income for the federal income tax, and the Social Security program receives part of those taxes.[20] Second, the Social Security program receives interest from the U.S. Treasury on its investments in special U.S. government obligations.

As the Managing Trustee of the Social Security trust funds, the Secretary of the Treasury is required by law to invest Social Security revenues in interest-bearing federal government securities held by the trust funds.[21] The revenues exchanged for the federal government securities are deposited into the general fund of the U.S. Treasury and are indistinguishable from revenues in the general fund that come from other sources. Because the assets held by the trust funds are federal government securities, the trust fund balance represents the amount of money owed to the Social Security trust funds by the general fund of the U.S. Treasury. Funds needed to pay Social Security benefits and administrative expenses come from the redemption of federal government securities held by the trust funds.[22]

Taxation of Social Security Benefits

Since 1984, Social Security benefits have been subject to the federal income tax. First, as part of the Social Security Amendments of 1983 (P.L. 98-21), Congress made up to 50% of a person's Social Security benefits subject to the federal income tax if he or she has modified adjusted gross income (AGI) above a specified threshold ($25,000 for an individual tax filer and $32,000 for a married couple filing jointly). Modified AGI is defined as the total income from all sources recognized for tax purposes plus certain otherwise tax-exempt income, including half of Social Security benefits. Tax revenues from this "first tier" of taxation are credited to the Social Security trust funds. In 2012, the trust funds received $27.3 billion (3.2% of total trust fund income) from this provision.[23]

Second, as part of the Omnibus Budget Reconciliation Act of 1993 (P.L. 103-66), Congress made up to 85% of a person's Social Security benefits subject to the federal income tax if he or she has modified AGI above a second higher threshold ($34,000 for an individual tax filer and $44,000 for a married couple filing jointly). Tax revenues from this "second tier" of taxation are credited to the Medicare HI trust fund. In 2012, the HI trust fund received $18.6 billion (7.7% of total trust fund income) from this provision.[24]

The income thresholds are fixed under current law (i.e., they are not adjusted for inflation or wage growth). Over time an increasing number of beneficiaries will be subject to the federal income tax on benefits.[25]

STATUS OF THE SOCIAL SECURITY TRUST FUNDS

Projections by the Social Security Board of Trustees (the trustees) show that Social Security expenditures will exceed *tax revenues* each year through the end of the 75-year valuation period (2087).[26] That is, Social Security will operate with annual *cash-flow deficits*. When interest income to the trust funds is taken into account, Social Security is projected to have a *total surplus* (tax revenues plus interest income will exceed expenditures) each year through 2020. The trustees project that the trust funds will have a positive balance until 2033, and Social Security benefits scheduled under current law can be paid in full and on time until then (until the accumulated assets held by the trust funds are exhausted). Although the trust funds are projected to have a positive balance until 2033 on a *combined basis*, the OASI trust fund is projected to be exhausted in 2035, and the DI trust fund is projected to be exhausted in 2016. Under current law, DI benefits could not be paid in full and on time following DI trust fund exhaustion in 2016. The trustees state, "the DI Trust Fund reserves become depleted in 2016, at which time continuing income to the DI Trust Fund would be sufficient to pay 80 percent of DI benefits. Therefore, legislative action is needed as soon as possible to address the DI program's financial imbalance. In the absence of a long-term solution, lawmakers could choose to reallocate a portion of the payroll tax rate between OASI and DI, as they did in 1994."[27]

Over the long run, the trustees project that Social Security expenditures will exceed income by about 20% *on average* over the next 75 years. Social Security's projected long-range funding shortfall is attributed primarily to demographic factors (such as lower fertility rates and increasing life expectancy) and program design features (such as a wage-indexed benefit formula and annual COLAs).[28]

At the end of 2012, the trust funds were credited with accumulated assets of $2.7 trillion. The trustees project that the trust fund balance will continue to grow over the next several years due to interest income, peaking at $2.9 trillion in current dollars ($2.4 trillion in constant 2013 dollars) at the end of 2020. Beginning in 2021, Social Security expenditures will exceed total income (tax revenues plus interest income) and the trust fund balance will begin to decline, until the accumulated trust fund assets are exhausted in 2033.

After trust fund exhaustion, the program would continue to operate with incoming Social Security receipts that are projected to be sufficient to pay 77% of benefits scheduled under current law in 2033 and 72% of scheduled benefits in 2087. Social Security does not have authority to borrow from the general fund of the Treasury. Therefore, the program cannot simply draw upon general revenues to make up the difference between incoming receipts and benefit payments when the program no longer has accumulated assets to draw upon. The Social Security Act does not state what would happen to the payment of benefits scheduled under current law in the event of Social Security trust fund exhaustion. Two possible scenarios are (1) the payment of full monthly benefits on a delayed schedule, or (2) the payment of partial (reduced) monthly benefits on time.[29]

Social Security Cash-Flow Surpluses and Deficits

From 1984 to 2009, Social Security generated surplus tax revenues (i.e., the program operated with annual cash-flow surpluses). Surplus tax revenues and interest income credited to the trust funds in the form of federal government securities contributed to a growing trust fund balance. Surplus Social Security tax revenues totaled $1.21 trillion (in current dollars) from 1984 to 2009. Beginning in 2010, however, the program began operating with annual cash-flow deficits, and the trustees project that Social Security tax revenues will remain below program expenditures each year throughout the 75-year projection period (2013-2087).

When Social Security operates with a cash-flow deficit, the trust funds redeem more federal securities than the amount of current Social Security tax revenues, relying in part on accumulated trust fund assets to pay benefits and administrative expenses. Because the federal securities held by the trust funds are redeemed with general revenues, this results in increased spending for

Social Security from the general fund. When there are no surplus governmental receipts, the federal government must raise the necessary funds by increasing taxes or other income; reducing other spending; borrowing from the public; or some combination of these measures.

With respect to the program's reliance on general revenues, it is important to note that the program is relying on revenues collected for Social Security purposes in previous years that were used by the federal government at the time for other (non-Social Security) spending needs and interest income earned on trust fund investments.

The program draws on those previously collected Social Security tax revenues and interest income (accumulated trust fund assets) when current Social Security tax revenues fall below current program expenditures.

Social Security Reform Debate

Social Security reform is an issue of ongoing interest to policymakers. For some advocates of reform, the focus is on restoring long-range solvency to the trust funds. For others, the focus is on constraining the projected growth in spending for entitlement programs—including Social Security, Medicare, and Medicaid—in the context of broader efforts to reduce growing federal budget deficits.

The Social Security reform debate reflects other policy objectives as well, such as improving the adequacy and equity of benefits, and different philosophical views about the role of the Social Security program and the federal government in providing retirement income. The debate reflects two fundamentally different approaches to reform. The *traditional approach* would maintain the current structure of the program (i.e., a defined benefit system funded on a pay-as-you-go basis) by making relatively modest changes, such as an increase in the retirement age or an increase in the taxable wage base. Generally, the goal of this approach is to preserve the social insurance nature of the program.

In contrast, the *personal savings and investment approach* would redesign the 1930s-era program to create a pre-funded system in which benefits would be based partially or entirely on personal savings and investments.[30]

SOCIAL SECURITY BENEFIT RULES

Social Security provides monthly cash benefits to retired or disabled workers and to the family members of retired, disabled, or deceased workers. The computation of a worker's primary insurance amount (PIA) is based on his or her earnings record in Social Security-covered employment. The worker's PIA is the initial monthly benefit amount payable at the full retirement age (i.e., before any adjustments for early or delayed retirement). Benefits paid to the family members of a worker are based on a percentage of the worker's PIA. The eligibility requirements for each category of benefits differ, as described below.

Full Retirement Age

Social Security retirement benefits are first payable to retired workers at the age of 62, subject to a permanent reduction for early retirement. The age at which full (or unreduced) retirement benefits are first payable is the full retirement age (FRA).[31] For most of the program's history, the FRA was 65. As part of the Social Security Amendments of 1983 (P.L. 98-21), Congress raised the FRA from 65 to 67. The 1983 law established a gradual phase-in from 65 to 67 over a 22-year period (2000 to 2022).

Specifically, persons born in 1938 or later are affected by the increase in the FRA (i.e., persons who become eligible for retirement benefits at age 62 in 2000 or later). The increase in the FRA will be fully phased-in for persons born in 1960 or later (i.e., persons who become eligible for retirement benefits at age 62 in 2022 or later). **Table 1** shows the scheduled increase in the FRA being phased-in under current law.[32]

Computation of a Social Security Retired-Worker Benefit

To be eligible for a Social Security retired-worker benefit, a person generally needs a minimum of 40 earnings credits, or 10 years of Social Security-covered employment (among other requirements).[33] A worker's initial monthly benefit is based on his or her 35 highest years of earnings, which are indexed to historical wage growth (earnings through age 60 are indexed; earnings thereafter are counted at nominal value). The 35 highest years of indexed earnings are divided by 35 to determine the worker's career-average annual earnings. The resulting amount is divided by 12 to determine the worker's average indexed monthly earnings (AIME). If a worker has fewer than 35 years of earnings in covered employment, years of no earnings are entered as zeroes in the computation, resulting in a lower AIME and therefore a lower monthly benefit.

Table 1. Increase in the Full Retirement Age Scheduled Under Current Law

Year of Birth	Full Retirement Age
1938	65 and 2 months
1939	65 and 4 months
1940	65 and 6 months
1941	65 and 8 months
1942	65 and 10 months
1943 to 1954	66
1955	66 and 2 months
1956	66 and 4 months
1957	66 and 6 months
1958	66 and 8 months
1959	66 and 10 months
1960 or later	67

Source: SSA, *2014 Social Security/SSI/Medicare Information*, January 7, 2014, available at http://www.socialsecurity.gov/legislation

The worker's PIA is determined by applying a formula to the AIME as shown in Table 2. First, the AIME is sectioned into three brackets (or segments) of earnings, which are divided by dollar amounts known as bend points. In 2014, the bend points are \$816 and \$4,917.[34] Three progressive replacement factors—90%, 32%, and 15%—are applied to the three brackets of AIME.[35] The three products derived from multiplying each replacement factor and bracket of AIME are added together. For workers who become eligible for retirement benefits (i.e., those who attain age 62), become disabled, or die in 2014, the PIA is determined as shown in the example in Table 2.

A worker's PIA increases each year from the year of eligibility (at age 62) to the year of benefit receipt based on the Social Security COLA. In addition, Social Security benefits already in payment increase each year based on the COLA.[36]

Table 2. Computation of a Worker's Primary Insurance Amount (PIA) in 2014 Based on an Illustrative AIME of $5,000

Factors	Three Brackets of AIME	PIA for Worker with an Illustrative AIME of $5,000
90%	first $816 of AIME, plus	$734.40
32%	AIME over $816 and through $4,917, plus	$1,312.30
15%	AIME over $4,917	$12.40
Total: Worker's PIA		$2,059.10

Source: Congressional Research Service (CRS).

Adjustments to Benefits Claimed Before or After the FRA

A worker's initial monthly benefit is equal to his or her PIA if he or she begins receiving benefits at the FRA. A worker's initial monthly benefit will be *less* than his or her PIA if he or she begins receiving benefits *before* the FRA, and it will be *greater* than his or her PIA if he or she begins receiving benefits *after* the FRA.

A retired-worker benefit is payable as early as the age of 62, however, the benefit will be permanently reduced to reflect the longer expected period of benefit receipt.

Retired-worker benefits are reduced by five-ninths of 1% (or 0.0056) of the worker's PIA for each month of entitlement before the FRA up to 36 months, for a reduction of about 6.7% a year. For each month of benefit entitlement before the FRA in excess of 36 months, retirement benefits are reduced by five-twelfths of 1% (or 0.0042), for a reduction of 5% a year.[37]

Workers who delay filing for benefits until after the FRA receive a delayed retirement credit (DRC). The DRC applies beginning with the month the worker attains the FRA and ending with the month before he or she attains the age of 70. Starting in 1990, the DRC increased until it reached 8% per year for workers born in 1943 or later (i.e., starting with those who attained age 62 in 2005 or age 66 in 2009).

The actuarial adjustment to benefits claimed before or after the FRA is intended to provide the worker with roughly the same total lifetime benefits, regardless of the age at which he or she begins receiving benefits. Therefore, if a worker claims benefits before the FRA, his or her monthly benefit is reduced to take into account the longer expected period of benefit receipt.

For a worker whose FRA is 66, the decision to claim benefits at the age of 62 results in a 25% reduction in his or her PIA. For a worker whose FRA is 67, the decision to claim benefits at the age of 62 results in a 30% reduction in his or her PIA.

Similarly, if a worker claims benefits after the FRA, his or her monthly benefit is increased to take into account the shorter expected period of benefit receipt.

Other Adjustments to Benefits (Including GPO and WEP)

Other adjustments to benefits may apply, such as those related to simultaneous entitlement to more than one type of Social Security benefit. Under the dual entitlement rule, a Social Security spousal benefit is reduced if the person is receiving a Social Security retired-worker benefit. Under the government pension offset (GPO), a Social Security spousal benefit is reduced if the spousal beneficiary is receiving a pension from work that was not covered by Social Security (a non-covered pension).[38]

Under the windfall elimination provision (WEP), the Social Security benefit formula is modified to reduce benefits for a worker beneficiary who has a pension from non-covered employment in federal, state, or local governments.[39] Under the retirement earnings test (RET), the monthly Social Security benefit is reduced for a person who is below the FRA and has wage or salary income above an annual dollar threshold (an annual exempt amount).[40]

Under the Social Security maximum family benefit provision (discussed below), the benefits of individual family members may be reduced to keep the total benefits payable to a family based on the worker's record within a specified limit.

Disabled-Worker Benefit

For Social Security disability benefits, "disability" is defined as the inability to engage in substantial gainful activity (SGA) by reason of a medically determinable physical or mental impairment expected to result in death or last at least 12 months. Generally, the worker must be unable to do any kind of work that exists in the national economy, taking into account age, education, and work experience. As noted above, a worker generally needs a minimum of 40 quarters of coverage for a Social Security retired-worker benefit.

A worker may qualify for Social Security disabled-worker benefits with fewer quarters of coverage, depending on the age at which the worker became disabled.

However, a minimum of six quarters of coverage is needed. Similarly, while the worker's 35 highest years of earnings are used to compute a retired-worker benefit, fewer years of earnings may be used to compute a disabled-worker benefit. Because a disabled worker's benefit is not reduced for entitlement before the FRA, a disabled worker's benefit is equal to his or her PIA.[41]

Benefits for the Worker's Family Members

Social Security may be viewed by some as a program that provides benefits only to retired or disabled workers; however, about 19% of Social Security beneficiaries are the dependents and survivors of retired, disabled, or deceased workers.[42]

Social Security benefits are payable to the spouse, divorced spouse, or child of a retired or disabled worker. Social Security benefits are also payable to the widow(er), divorced widow(er), child, or parent of a deceased worker. In addition, in the case of a deceased worker, benefits are payable to the mother or father of a deceased worker's child when the child is under the age of 16 or disabled and entitled to a Social Security child's benefit based on the worker's record.[43]

Benefits payable to family members are equal to a specified percentage of the worker's PIA, subject to a maximum family benefit amount. For example, the spouse of a retired worker may receive up to 50% of the retired worker's PIA, and the widow(er) of a deceased worker may receive up to 100% of the deceased worker's PIA.

Benefits paid to family members may be subject to adjustments based on the person's age at entitlement, receipt of his or her own Social Security retired-worker benefit, and other factors, as described above.

Table 3 provides a summary of Social Security benefits payable to family members of a retired, disabled, or deceased worker, including basic eligibility requirements and basic benefit amounts before any applicable adjustments are made (such as for the maximum family benefit amount).[44]

Maximum Family Benefit Amount

The total amount of Social Security benefits payable to a family based on a retired or deceased worker's record is capped by the maximum family benefit amount.

The maximum family benefit varies from 150% to 188% of the retired or deceased worker's PIA. It cannot be exceeded regardless of the number of beneficiaries entitled to benefits on the worker's record.[45] If the sum of all benefits based on the worker's record exceeds the maximum family benefit amount, each dependent's or survivor's benefit is reduced in equal proportion to bring the total amount of benefits within the family maximum. For the family of a worker who attains the age of 62 in 2014, or dies in 2014 before attaining the age of 62, the total amount of benefits payable is limited to

- 150% of the first $1,042 of the worker's PIA, plus
- 272% of the worker's PIA over $1,042 and through $1,505, plus
- 134% of the worker's PIA over $1,505 and through $1,962, plus
- 175% of the worker's PIA over $1,962.

The dollar amounts in the maximum family benefit formula ($1,042, $1,505, and $1,962 in 2014) are indexed to average wage growth, as in the regular benefit formula. A different family maximum applies in the case of a disabled worker. For the family of a worker who is entitled to disability benefits, the maximum family benefit is the lesser of 85% of the worker's AIME or 150% of the worker's PIA. In no case, however, can the family benefit be less than 100% of the worker's PIA.[46]

SOCIAL SECURITY BENEFICIARIES

In November 2013, there were 57.9 million Social Security beneficiaries. As shown in Table 4, retired-worker and disabled-worker beneficiaries accounted for 80.7% of the beneficiary population. The largest single category of beneficiaries was retired workers (65.3%), with an average monthly benefit of $1,273.91. The second-largest category was disabled workers (15.4%), with an average monthly benefit of $1,129.65. Family members of retired, disabled, or deceased workers accounted for the remainder of the beneficiary population (19.3%). Table 4 provides a detailed breakdown of the Social Security beneficiary population in November 2013.

Table 3. Social Security Benefits for the Worker's Family Members

Basis for Entitlement	Basic Eligibility Requirements	Basic Benefit Amount Before Any Applicable Adjustments
Spouse	At least age 62, or Any age if caring for the child of a retired or disabled worker. The child must be under the age of 16 or disabled and entitled to a child's benefit based on the worker's record. The worker on whose record benefits are based must be receiving benefits.	50% of worker's PIA
Divorced Spouse (if divorced individual was married to the worker for at least 10 years before the divorce became final and is currently unmarried)	At least age 62 Generally, the worker on whose record benefits are based must be receiving benefits. However, a divorced spouse may receive benefits on the worker's record if the worker is eligible for (but not receiving) benefits and the divorce has been final for at least two years. (Note: A divorced spouse who is under the age of 62 is not eligible for spousal benefits even if he or she is caring for the child of a retired or disabled worker and the child is entitled to benefits based on the worker's record.)	50% of worker's PIA

Table 3. (Continued)

Basis for Entitlement	Basic Eligibility Requirements	Basic Benefit Amount Before Any Applicable Adjustments
Widow(er) & Divorced Widow(er) (if divorced individual was married to the worker for at least 10 years before the divorce became final and did not remarry before age 60)	At least age 60	100% of worker's PIA
Disabled Widow(er) & Divorced Disabled Widow(er) (if divorced individual was married to the worker for at least 10 years before the divorce became final and did not remarry before age 50)	At least age 50 The qualifying disability must have occurred: (1) before or within seven years of the worker's death; (2) within seven years of having been previously entitled to benefits on the worker's record as a widow(er) with a child in his or her care; or (3) within seven years of having been previously entitled to benefits as a disabled widow(er) that ended because the qualifying disability ended (whichever is later).	100% of worker's PIA
Mothers and Fathers	Surviving parent of any age who cares for the deceased worker's child, when the child is either under age 16 or disabled and entitled to a child's benefit based on the deceased worker's record. To receive mother's or father's benefits, the person must be unmarried and not entitled to widow(er)'s benefits.	75% of deceased worker's PIA (subject to the maximum family benefit amount)

Basis for Entitlement	Basic Eligibility Requirements	Basic Benefit Amount Before Any Applicable Adjustments
Parents	At least age 62 and has not married since the worker's death. The parent must have been receiving at least one-half of his or her support from the worker at the time of the worker's death or, if the worker had a period of disability which continued until death, at the beginning of the period of disability.	If one parent is entitled to benefits: 82.5% of deceased worker's PIA If two parents are entitled to benefits: 75% of deceased worker's PIA (for each) (subject to the maximum family benefit amount)
Child	A child (including a dependent, unmarried biological child, adopted child, stepchild, and, in some cases, grandchild) of a retired, disabled, or deceased worker who was fully or currently insured at the time of death. The child must be (1) under age 18; (2) a full-time elementary or secondary student under age 19; or (3) a disabled person aged 18 or older whose disability began before age 22.	50% of worker's PIA for child of a retired or disabled worker 75% of deceased worker's PIA for child of a deceased worker (subject to the maximum family benefit amount)

Source: Congressional Research Service (CRS).

Notes: The table shows the minimum eligibility age for each type of benefit (i.e., the age at which benefits are first payable on a reduced basis). The maximum family benefit may apply, reducing the benefit received by each family member on a proportional basis. The maximum family benefit varies from 150% to 188% of a retired or deceased worker's PIA. For the family of a worker who is entitled to disability benefits, the maximum family benefit is the lesser of 85% of the worker's AIME or 150% of the worker's PIA, but no less than 100% of the worker's PIA. Other benefit adjustments may apply.

Table 4. Social Security Beneficiaries, by Type, November 2013

Type of Beneficiary	Number of Beneficiaries (in thousands)	Percentage of Beneficiaries	Total Monthly Benefits ($ in millions)	Average Monthly Benefit (in dollars)
All beneficiaries	57,917	100.0%	$67,425	$1,164.18
Old-Age and Survivors	46,935	81.0	56,645	1,206.87
Insurance				
Retirement benefits	40,744	70.4	50,044	1,228.25
- Retired workers	37,835	65.3	48,198	1,273.91
- Spouses of retired workers	2,287	3.9	1,459	637.78
- Children of retired workers	622	1.1	387	622.27
Survivor benefits	6,191	10.7	6,600	1,066.14
- Children of deceased workers	1,891	3.3	1,515	801.23
- Widowed mothers and fathers	151	0.3	137	906.06
- Nondisabled widow(er)s	3,890	6.7	4,765	1,224.95
- Disabled widow(er)s	257	0.4	182	706.60
- Parents of deceased workers	1	a	1	1,077.42
Disability Insurance	10,981	19.0	10,780	981.70
- Disabled workers	8,941	15.4	10,100	1,129.65
- Spouses of disabled workers	157	0.3	48	303.53
- Children of disabled workers	1,883	3.3	633	335.99

Source: Table is reproduced from SSA, *Monthly Statistical Snapshot, November 2013*, Table 2. See the latest edition of the *Monthly Statistical Snapshot* at http://www.socialsecurity.gov/policy index.html.

a. Indicates a value less than 0.05%.

End Notes

[1] Social Security Administration (SSA), *Monthly Statistical Snapshot, November 2013*, Table 2. See the latest edition of the *Monthly Statistical Snapshot* at http://www.socialsecurity.gov /policy/docs/quickfacts/stat_snapshot/index.html. Details may not sum to totals due to rounding.

[2] Currently, 93% of workers in paid employment or self-employment are covered by Social Security. (SSA, *2014 Social Security/SSI/Medicare Information*, January 7, 2014, at http://www.socialsecurity.gov/legislation 2014factsheet.pdf.)

[3] The annual limit on covered wages and net self-employment income subject to the Social Security payroll tax (the taxable wage base) is adjusted annually based on average wage growth, if a Social Security cost-of-living adjustment (COLA) is payable.

[4] In 2011, there was a temporary 2 percentage point reduction in the Social Security payroll tax rate for workers under P.L. 111-312. The temporary reduction was extended through February 2012 under P.L. 112-78, and further extended through December 2012 under P.L. 112-96. For more information, see CRS Report R41648, *Social Security: Temporary Payroll Tax Reduction*, by Dawn Nuschler.

[5] In this report, the OASI and DI trust funds are referred to on a combined basis as the Social Security trust funds.

[6] SSA, *Trust Fund Data*, http://www.ssa.gov/OACT/STATS/table4a3.html.

[7] P.L. 271, 74th Congress.

[8] P.L. 379, 76th Congress.

[9] The DI program was established by the Social Security Amendments of 1956 (P.L. 880, 84th Congress). The program became known as the Old-Age, Survivors, and Disability Insurance (OASDI) program, the formal name for Social Security.

[10] Congress has increased the Social Security payroll tax rate many times over the program's history. The payroll tax rate under current law (12.4%) was established by the Social Security Amendments of 1983 (P.L. 98-21). P.L. 98-21 increased the payroll tax rate gradually from 11.4% in 1984 to 12.4% in 1990.

[11] The taxable wage base amounts ($3,000 and $117,000) are in current dollars. The most recent legislative change to the Social Security taxable wage base was in 1977. The Social Security Amendments of 1977 (P.L. 95-216) established ad-hoc increases in the taxable wage base for 1979, 1980, and 1981, followed by a return to automatic wage indexation for 1982 and subsequent years.

[12] For example, the Social Security Amendments of 1965 (P.L. 89-97) established benefits for divorced wives aged 62 or older.

[13] See the Social Security Amendments of 1972 (P.L. 92-603). For more information, see CRS Report 94-803, *Social Security: Cost-of-Living Adjustments*, by Gary Sidor.

[14] See the Social Security Amendments of 1977 (P.L. 95-216).

[15] Following the Social Security Amendments of 1983 (P.L. 98-21), projections showed the re-emergence of long-range deficits as a result of changes in actuarial methods and assumptions and because program changes had been evaluated with respect to their effect on the *average* 75-year deficit. That is, while program changes were projected to restore trust fund solvency *on average* over the 75-year projection period, a period of surplus years was followed by a period of deficit years. As time passed, the inclusion of additional deficit years in the 75-year valuation period resulted in a return to projected long-range deficits.

[16] For more information, see CRS Report RL33544, *Social Security Reform: Current Issues and Legislation*, by Dawn Nuschler.

[17] The Patient Protection and Affordable Care Act (ACA, P.L. 111-148) imposed an additional Medicare HI tax of 0.9 percentage point on high-income workers with wages over $200,000 for single filers and $250,000 for joint filers, effective for taxable years beginning in 2013.

[18] Self-employed individuals are required to pay Social Security payroll taxes if they have annual net earnings of $400 or more. Only 92.35% of net self-employment income (up to the annual limit) is taxable.

[19] If a self-employed person does not pay him/herself wages, SECA taxes are paid annually on the Internal Revenue Service Form 1040 (U.S. Individual Income Tax Return). If a self-employed person does pay him/herself wages, FICA taxes are paid during the year along with any FICA tax payments for his or her employees.

[20] The taxes associated with including Social Security benefits in federal taxable income go to the Social Security trust funds and the Medicare HI trust fund. See CRS Report RL32552, *Social Security: Calculation and History of Taxing Benefits*, by Christine Scott.

[21] Social Security Act, Title II, §201(d). For more information, see SSA, Office of the Chief Actuary, Actuarial Note Number 142, *Social Security Trust Fund Investment Policies and Practices*, by Jeffrey L. Kunkel, January 1999, at http://www.ssa.gov/OACT/NOTES /n1990s.html.

[22] SSA, *Trust Fund FAQs*, http://www.socialsecurity.gov/OACT/ProgData/ fundFAQ.html.

[23] The 2013 Annual Report of the Board of Trustees of the Federal Old-Age and Survivors Insurance and Federal Disability Insurance Trust Funds, May 31, 2013, at http://www.socialsecurity.gov/OACT/TR/2013/tr2013.pdf. (Hereinafter cited as 2013 Annual Report of the Social Security Board of Trustees.) See Table III.A3 on page 32.

[24] *Status of the Social Security and Medicare Programs: A Summary of the 2013 Annual Reports*, Social Security and Medicare Boards of Trustees, May 31, 2013, page 2, http://www.socialsecurity.gov/OACT/TRSUM/tr13summary.pdf.

[25] For more information, see CRS Report RL32552, *Social Security: Calculation and History of Taxing Benefits*, by Christine Scott.

[26] Projections cited in this CRS report are based on the intermediate (or "best estimate") assumptions of the 2013 Annual Report of the Social Security Board of Trustees and refer to the OASI and DI trust funds on a combined basis. For more information on the trust fund projections, see CRS Report RL33028, *Social Security: The Trust Fund*, by Dawn Nuschler and Gary Sidor.

[27] 2013 Annual Report of the Social Security Board of Trustees, p. 4. In 1994, the reallocation of the payroll tax rate between OASI and DI was part of the Social Security Domestic Employment Reform Act of 1994 (P.L. 103-387). For more information on the status of the DI trust fund, see CRS Report R43318, *Social Security Disability Insurance (DI) Trust Fund: Background and Solvency Issues*, by William R. Morton.

[28] A wage-indexed benefit formula allows initial monthly benefits for successive groups of new beneficiaries to keep pace with increases in the standard of living. An annual COLA for benefits already in payment allows benefits for current beneficiaries to keep pace with increases in prices.

[29] For more information, see CRS Report RL32822, *Social Security Reform: Legal Analysis of Social Security Benefit Entitlement Issues*, by Kathleen S. Swendiman and Thomas J. Nicola, and CRS Report RL33514, *Social Security: What Would Happen If the Trust Funds Ran Out?*, by Christine Scott.

[30] For more information, see CRS Report RL33544, *Social Security Reform: Current Issues and Legislation*, by Dawn Nuschler.

[31] The full retirement age is also called the normal retirement age (NRA).

[32] For more information, see CRS Report R41962, *Fact Sheet: The Social Security Retirement Age*, by Gary Sidor.

[33] A worker may earn up to four earnings credits (or quarters of coverage, QCs) per calendar year. In 2014, a worker earns one QC for each $1,200 of covered earnings, up to a maximum of four QCs for earnings of $4,800 or more.

[34] The bend points in the benefit formula are indexed to average wage growth under current law.

[35] The replacement factors in the benefit formula are fixed under current law.

[36] A Social Security COLA was not payable in 2010 and 2011. For more information, see CRS Report 94-803, *Social Security: Cost-of-Living Adjustments*, by Gary Sidor.

[37] The early retirement reduction for *spousal benefits* is different. Spousal benefits claimed before the FRA are reduced by 25/36 of 1% (or 0.0069) for each month of entitlement before the FRA, up to 36 months, and by five-twelfths of 1% (or 0.0042) for each month of entitlement before the FRA in excess of 36 months. The reduction is applied to the base spousal benefit, which is 50% of the worker's PIA. The spousal benefit is not reduced for entitlement before the FRA if the spouse is caring for a qualifying child.

[38] For more information on the dual entitlement rule and the GPO, see CRS Report RL32453, *Social Security: The Government Pension Offset (GPO)*, by Christine Scott.

[39] For more information on the WEP, see CRS Report 98-35, *Social Security: The Windfall Elimination Provision (WEP)*, by Christine Scott.

[40] For more information on the RET, see CRS Report R41242, *Social Security Retirement Earnings Test: How Earnings Affect Benefits*, by Dawn Nuschler.

[41] For more information, see CRS Report RL32279, *Primer on Disability Benefits: Social Security Disability Insurance (SSDI) and Supplemental Security Income (SSI)*, by Umar Moulta-Ali.

[42] SSA, *Monthly Statistical Snapshot, November 2013*, Table 2. See the latest edition of the *Monthly Statistical Snapshot* at http://www.socialsecurity. gov/policy/docs/quickfacts/stat_ snapshot/index.html.

[43] To receive mother's/father's benefits, the person must be unmarried and must not be entitled to widow(er)'s benefits.

[44] For related information, see CRS Report RS22294, *Social Security Survivors Benefits*, by Scott D. Szymendera.

[45] Social Security Act, Title II, §203.

[46] Benefits for a divorced beneficiary are not taken into account for purposes of the family maximum. SSA, Program Operations Manual System (POMS), Section RS 00615.682, "Family Benefits Where a Divorced Spouse or a Surviving Divorced Spouse is Entitled," available at https://secure.ssa.gov/apps10/ poms.nsf/lnx/0300615682.

INDEX

D

E

F

G

H

I

J

L

M

N

O

P

Q

R

S

T

U

V

W